Celtic Advent

The Bible Reading Fellowship
15 The Chambers, Vineyard
Abingdon OX14 3FE
brf.org.uk

The Bible Reading Fellowship (BRF) is a Registered Charity (233280)

ISBN 978 0 85746 744 7
First published 2018
10 9 8 7 6 5 4 3 2 1 0

Cover and inside illustrations by Rebecca J Hall

Acknowledgements
Unless otherwise acknowledged, scripture quotations are from The New Revised Standard Version of the Bible, Anglicised edition, copyright © 1989, 1995 by the Division of Christian Education of the National Council of the Churches of Christ in the United States of America. Used by permission. All rights reserved.

Scripture quotations taken from the Holy Bible, New Living Translation, copyright © 1996, 2004, 2007, 2013. Used by permission of Tyndale House Publishers, Inc., Carol Stream, Illinois 60188. All rights reserved.

Scripture taken from the New King James Version®. Copyright © 1982 by Thomas Nelson. Used by permission. All rights reserved.

Scripture quotations are taken from *The Message*, copyright © 1993, 1994, 1995, 1996, 2000, 2001, 2002 by Eugene H. Peterson. Used by permission of NavPress. All rights reserved. Represented by Tyndale House Publishers, Inc.

p. 76: Extract taken from the song 'Everything' by Tim Hughes. Copyright © Thankyou Music. Adm. by Capitol CMG Publishing worldwide excl. UK & Europe, admin by Integrity Music, part of the David C Cook family, songs@integritymusic.com.

Every effort has been made to trace and contact copyright owners for material used in this resource. We apologise for any inadvertent omissions or errors, and would ask those concerned to contact us so that full acknowledgement can be made in the future.

A catalogue record for this book is available from the British Library

Printed and bound by CPI Group (UK) Ltd, Croydon CR0 4YY

Celtic Advent

40 days of devotions to Christmas

David Cole

Acknowledgements

Thank you to all those who have been a part of the creation of this book, especially Simon Reed for his painstaking readings of the first drafts. Thank you to all those throughout my life who have helped make Christmastime a special and sacred time for me.

Contents

The third coming of Christ

Celebrating the Christmas feast and winter celebrations

Introduction

Christmas! For many of us, Christmas is a wonderful time of year where we see those we love and share in jollity, mirth and the giving and receiving of gifts. (We may even venture out to church!) All this is right and good; God is a God of fun and celebrations! When God first spoke to the Hebrew people after the exodus about becoming a people of YHWH, there were over a dozen feasts and celebrations as part of it. More have been added over the years, such as Hanukkah, the Jewish winter festival. Feast, celebration, joy and happiness have always been a part of God's plan for the people who make up the body of followers and believers.

However, when we read the Old Testament, it is clear that the feasts didn't just happen; there was a time of preparation beforehand as well. In the time leading up to the feast or celebration where the people would get themselves ready to celebrate, they would prepare themselves inwardly as well as outwardly for the focus of the feast. This is exactly what Advent is. The word itself comes from the Latin *adventus*, which means 'arrival'. Like the arrival of any other baby, the waiting for the arrival of the birth of Jesus was not, and is not, idle anticipation, but active waiting.

Advent has two traditional start dates, depending upon your understanding. There is the traditional church date of the fourth Sunday before Christmas; and then there is the first day of December, when you open the first door of your Advent calendar. But in the ancient church of Britain and Ireland (commonly referred to today as the 'Celtic church') there was another date – 15 November, the eve of 15 November in fact. The reason for this date was because 15 November is 40 days before Christmas (including Sundays, unlike the 40 days of Lent), and the Celtic church believed in the same significance of numbers as the Jewish faith. The Celtic church referred to the period of Advent as the 'lesser Lent' and believed that the period for preparation was important, just like the preparation of Lent leading up to Easter.

It is traditionally believed that the Celtic church, during this 40-day Advent, focused on what is called the three comings of Christ. The first was the incarnation, which is what Christmas is all about; the second was the coming of Christ into our own selves. This was not just a single event for the Celtic Christians, what the modern church may call 'conversion' or 'becoming a Christian', but it was a continual activity in every part of our lives on a daily basis. It might even need to happen multiple times a day, and in every decision that is made. This isn't about eternal salvation; this is about Christ being intrinsically involved and interwoven in every part and aspect of our everyday lives. The third coming is the return of Christ at the end of all things as we know it, as described in the book of Revelation.

Over the 40 days of Celtic Advent, following in the tradition of the ancient Celtic church, we will discover what it means to prepare for the coming of the Christ by focusing upon the three comings of Christ.

We will begin with five days looking at the concept of Advent; then we will spend ten days looking at the coming of Christ incarnate as a baby, as described in the gospels. After that, we will spend ten days on the coming of Christ into our lives, both the first time it happened and the continual need for it to happen throughout our lives. Moving from here, we will look at the coming of Christ at the end, what Christians often call 'the second coming'. Finally, we will spend five days looking at Christmas itself as a celebration.

As Celtic Advent began on the evening of 15 November, it is suggested that you use these devotions in this book in the evenings. This means that your first reading will be on the evening of 15 November and your final reading will consequently be on the evening of 24 December, leading you right into the night vigil or midnight mass before Christmas day.

As you journey through this book over Advent in the lead-up to Christmas, I pray that you will be drawn closer to God and that, consequently, as it says in James 4:8, God will draw close to you, so that this Christmas you will have a close encounter with Christ and know the joy of God in the celebrations which surround us all.

David Cole

The concept of Advent: preparations for the arrival

15 November

Advent is a time of waiting: not an idle waiting, but an active and pragmatic waiting. For the Celtic Christians, it was a time to look both towards the coming Christ and also within themselves. It was a time to 'prepare the way for the Lord; make straight… a highway for our God' (Isaiah 40:3), both within themselves and also in the world in which they lived.

Preparation is an important part of any planning. When Celtic Christians were to do anything, they would spend time (often a period of 40 days) in prayer and preparation before they began. They did this when monastic centres were to be planted, when missions were to be undertaken or even when they were to go out on adventures!

Brendon the Navigator, for example, the sixth-century Irish monk, before he set off on his most famous voyage from the north coast of Ireland to arrive in what is now called America, spent 40 days in prayer and preparation, along with other monks. Brendon had been so inspired by Barinthus in his tale about the 'Island of Delights'[1] that he decided he would venture there. So Brendan chose seven monks from his community and, in a closed meeting, said to them:

> My most beloved fellow-warriors, I look to you for advice and help, for my heart and all my thoughts are united in a single desire. I have resolved in my heart, if only it be God's will, to seek that Promised Land of the Saints, of which Barinthus has spoken. How does this seem to you, and what advice do you wish to give me?[2]

The monks all agreed together that they would follow Brendan in whatever he believed was right. So 'Brendan and those who were with him completed a 40-day fast, in three-day periods, before they set out.'[3]

Over the next few days, we will be looking at the concept of Advent as a time of preparation, leading us into the following weeks where we will look more deeply into the three comings of Christ.

Contemplation

As we begin this journey into Advent, start by setting your heart in the right direction. Spend a few moments just sitting quietly and focusing on the coming season – not on all the busyness of what needs to be done, but on the spiritual significance of what is coming up. From the very depths of your inner self, commit this time into God's hands and into the divine flow.

Reading

> He went into all the region around the Jordan, proclaiming a baptism of repentance for the forgiveness of sins, as it is written in the book of the words of the prophet Isaiah,
>
> 'The voice of one crying out in the wilderness:
> "Prepare the way of the Lord,
> make his paths straight.
> Every valley shall be filled,
> and every mountain and hill shall be made low,
> and the crooked shall be made straight,
> and the rough ways made smooth;
> and all flesh shall see the salvation of God."'
>
> LUKE 3:3–6

Prayer

God of all gods, as I begin these 40 days of preparation, I commit my life to you. I commit the path ahead to you. I commit myself to be open to whatever change you call me to make. Amen

16 November

In the story of Brendan, we discovered that he had a great desire: something burning in his heart that he wanted to do. He tells his monks that 'my heart and all my thoughts are united in a single desire'. This single desire was the great sailing adventure across the unknown waters into the distant nothingness which lay beyond (as far as they knew). This desire had caught Brendon's imagination and he was off in a flow of enthusiasm about this great adventure. I wonder if you have ever had such an experience, where something has caught your heart in such a way that you go off in an almost (or sometimes fully) uncontrollable flow of 'this is what I want'. Enthusiasm and passion for something, especially if we feel that it is a call from God, is not a bad thing. Perhaps there needs to be more of that kind of passionate desire for things within the body of Christ.

But let us pause for a moment and take another glance back at the statement of Brendon to his fellow monks. After saying that his heart and thoughts were united in this single desire, expressing this passion which dwelt within him, he then says, 'I have resolved in my heart, if only it be God's will…' Let us just pause a moment and look at this. This is such an important moment in all things, especially when we have a desire that is overwhelming our heart with a passion. It is great to have a passionate desire for something, but it is equally important that we pause, take a moment and just check that we go ahead 'if only it be God's will'. This is the time to gently lay down our passion and desire, and to dwell quietly in God's presence to discover whether this desire is something of our own self-induced will or ego, whether it is something which we feel pushed into by other people or whether it is truly something which is divinely inspired.

The story of Brendon tells us that he did two things to discover this. Firstly, he asked others what they thought, and then they all spent time in prayerful consideration. Both of these actions are good, sage advice as part of our preparations when we are at the cusp of something new that we have an uncontrollable desire to do. Ask advice from others; then spend time in prayer about it.

Contemplation

When you begin something, or when you approach a significant project or venture, how much time do you put into prayerful preparation? Do you just launch straight into something, hoping that God will be with you and bless it? Or do you sit and prayerfully consider what the divine plan might be? And do you ask the advice of others too?

Spend time dwelling with God over what significant aspects of life might be coming up in the future. Then just spend time dwelling in the divine presence over them.

Reading

> And let the peace of Christ rule in your hearts, to which indeed you were called in the one body. And be thankful. Let the word of Christ dwell in you richly; teach and admonish one another in all wisdom.
>
> COLOSSIANS 3:15–16a

Prayer

Gracious God, thank you for giving me the passion to do great things. Thank you that you desire for me to follow your will. In all that lies before me in the future, in all that excites me, cause me to pause to check that the path I am about to step upon is the one you lay before me. Surround me with those who will give wise counsel, and may I be drawn into great things for you. Amen

17 November

In our dining room at home, we have a small framed blackboard with a tray of chalk at the bottom. More often than not, the blackboard has a list on it: a list of what needs doing; a to-do list. We all have these lists. The likelihood is that you have one for all the preparations you have to make before Christmas. But how do you order the priorities on these lists? And do you have prayer on your to-do list? Or is that something which gets squeezed in at some point in the midst of all the busy preparations?

The physical everyday tasks seem to dominate the priorities in our preconditioned society over those things which we might deem spiritual. To 'get on with things' is the way of western culture. But this can often be detrimental to the outcome of what we do.

When Aidan first arrived in the kingdom of Northumbria and King Oswald gave him the island of Lindisfarne as a base, there was a great deal to do: preparing the land for building, grazing and crops; building shelters and houses; building a chapel; creating a working farm to enable them to be self-sufficient; and a great deal more. All the practicalities of setting up a monastic centre lay ahead of Aidan and his twelve monks who had recently travelled from Iona, let alone the expectation from the king and those still on Iona to get out and take the gospel to the people. That's what they had been called here to do, after all. They needed to prioritise.

Aidan, as bishop in charge, was the one to make the to-do list in priority order. The monks waited to see what would be the first and most important task. The chapel? Surely that would be the first thing. But what about the cells for the monks to live in? That was also important. What would Aidan do? What would be the first thing on the list? Aidan looked at his monks as they waited in anticipation of his word and instruction. He looked around at the place they were standing, knowing all that needed to be done. Aidan made a choice.

> Though there were many tasks, 40 days were set aside for prayer and for the dedication and preparation of the site as a 'city of God'. During this time silence was often stronger than words and stillness more powerful than action. An area was marked out which would surround their future [monastic site]... the monks were not just clearing the land, but cleansing it from its past... Once the foundations of prayer had been laid, the monks built their own cells.[4]

In this action of setting aside a time for prayer first, Bishop Aidan ensured that everything they were going to do in the future, both the practical work of keeping a monastic centre going and the time spent in mission, as well as time spent with God, was set upon the foundation of prayer and guided by the Holy Spirit. The foundations we set our practical activities and everyday chores upon can have a significant impact on how these things turn out.

Contemplation

When you create your to-do lists, when you prioritise what you are going to do and how you will structure your day, do you begin with a time of prayer?

Do you consider God as a part of all the things which fill your lists of practical activities and necessities? Or do you just get on with it yourself?

Draw to mind any such lists which you currently have or might be about to make. Pause for a short time and draw God into the list. Ensure that God is a part of your day's practicalities, and in all the preparation which you have listed for the coming season leading up to Christmas.

Reading

> And whatever you do, in word or deed, do everything in the name of the Lord Jesus, giving thanks to God the Father through him.
> COLOSSIANS 3:17

Prayer

Holy God, as I step into all that I have to do today, and over the days which lay ahead, remind me that you are there with me, and that you desire to be a part of my everyday life. May I begin all things by focusing on you, to set the ground; may I continue through all things focused on you ensuring you are at the centre of all I do; and may I end each task focused on you, knowing that I have completed it with you. Amen

18 November

For the last two days looking at Advent, or the preparation leading up to Christmas, we will look at something from the beautiful Celtic and Anglo-Saxon illuminated scriptures: a particular page from both the Book of Kells and the Lindisfarne Gospels. We will look at the 'Chi-Rho' (Key-Roe) pages, sometimes known as the 'Incarnation Initial'.[5] In both of these beautifully created gospel books, the Chi-Rho page appears at the beginning of Matthew's gospel, the first gospel. In some sense, this artwork was an entranceway, a doorway, into the gospel – a contemplative and meditative way into the story of the life of Christ.

The Chi and the Rho are the first two letters of the Greek spelling of Christ (the 'Ch' and the 'R'). The 'Ch' is shaped a little like an English 'X'. It is, in fact, this Chi which adorns some modern abbreviations of the word Christmas, the Greek letter X representing the whole word 'Christ'. So, when you see, or write yourself, 'Xmas' instead of the full 'Christmas', you are, in fact, drawing on a very ancient concept which is celebrated in the Book of Kells and the Lindisfarne Gospels, from the pages which are perhaps the most elaborate in the books and which had the most time spent upon them. Writing 'Xmas' is not 'crossing out Christ from Christmas', as I have heard it put by some folk, but it is actually writing exactly the same thing (some may even argue writing it more intelligently, using Greek).

The Chi Rho page in both of these gospels contains beautiful artwork which would have been painstakingly meditated upon. We see beautiful swirls and elaborate knotwork. We see people, faces and angels, as well as other creatures such as moths, cats, rats and birds. The inside of the Chi in the Lindisfarne Gospels is an unbroken collection of many interwoven birds with bodies and legs as Celtic knotwork. It is worth stopping and spending some time looking carefully and contemplatively at these pages, either by getting a book with them in or by pulling up the pictures on the internet.

With the Chi Rho pages preceding the first gospel, with them being like an entranceway, a doorway, into the story of the life of Christ, I like to think of these pages from these books (and there are numerous other such books, such as the Gospel of Chad for example) as perhaps the Celtic understanding of the 'Cosmic Christ'; that is, that although Christ became incarnate at the birth which Christians celebrate at Christmas, he had always existed within the godhead, as part of the infinite Trinity from before the creation of the world and time.

Contemplation

Get hold of a picture of the Chi Rho page from either the Book of Kells or the Lindisfarne Gospels. As you spend time gazing upon it, contemplate the concept of the Cosmic Christ: the fact that Christ existed, uncreated, before all things as part of the Trinity godhead.

Follow the flow of the knotwork and swirls and allow your imagination to feel what it may have been like for the Cosmic Christ to flow into human form from the supernatural realm.

As you gaze upon the creatures and faces within these pages, imagine the Cosmic Christ becoming a part of the creation he had been a part of producing.

Reading

In the beginning was the Word, and the Word was with God, and the Word was God. He was in the beginning with God. All things came into being through him, and without him not one thing came into being. What has come into being in him was life, and the life was the light of all people. The light shines in the darkness, and the darkness did not overcome it.

There was a man sent from God, whose name was John. He came as a witness to testify to the light, so that all might believe through him. He himself was not the light, but he came to testify to the light. The true light, which enlightens everyone, was coming into the world.

He was in the world, and the world came into being through him; yet the world did not know him. He came to what was his own, and his own people did not accept him. But to all who received him, who believed in his name, he gave power to become children of God, who were born, not of blood or of the will of the flesh or of the will of man, but of God.

And the Word became flesh and lived among us, and we have seen his glory, the glory as of a father's only son, full of grace and truth.

JOHN 1:1–14

Prayer

Cosmic Christ, as I prepare to enter the story of your incarnation, may I know the sense of your presence with me. As the beauty and intricate details on the Chi Rho pages flow, may I know a sense of your Spirit flowing within me. Draw me into the beauty and detail of creation. May I see as you see. May I feel as you feel. May I love as you love. Amen

19 November

As well as the Chi Rho monogram preceding the story of the birth of Christ, there is something else on these pages too. The Lindisfarne Gospels shows this much more than the Book of Kells, as the Lindisfarne Gospels has more of it, but it is there in a smaller way in the Book of Kells; Chi Rho page too. The Chi Rho page was not just a nice piece of artwork, like the carpet pages; it was, in fact, the beginning of Matthew's gospel.

Matthew's gospel begins with a genealogy of the line which Jesus came from: his ancestry. Some of these words are written on the Chi Rho pages.

These words, which follow on from the beautiful Chi Rho illuminations, help us to further draw on that concept of the ineffable Cosmic Christ becoming incarnate and taking on human form. Simply compare the size and beauty of the Chi Rho illumination to the small wording written in 'ordinariness'. Jesus had a family line, an earthly ancestry, or at least he was born into a family line. This, of course, was important to fulfil Old Testament prophesies of the coming Messiah, as we can see with the names of such Judaic giants as Abraham, Isaac, Jacob, Judah and King David being part of the ancestral line for example.

But it is not just a list of names of either Joseph's or Mary's ancestry into which Jesus was born, just to fulfil Old Testament prophecies. This list on the Chi Rho pages does something more than that. For me, these two aspects of these pages draw together the divinity and the humanity of Jesus Christ. Not two separate things, but one interwoven being, unlike any other who had ever lived before or since – the divine incarnate. God in a body.

Ancestry was also important in the Celtic and Anglo-Saxon cultures. Often, introductions would be given as 'so and so, son or daughter of so and so'. The line from which you came was an important aspect of these cultures. Many of the Celtic saints, of course, in a similar but very much less significant way to Christ, gave up a royal or noble family line to become monks or nuns. Columba, for example, his biographer Adamnan tells us, came from the family line of the High Kings of Ireland. He may not have ever made it to the throne itself (although who knows with the amount of battles that took place, killing off king after king), but we know he was from that royal line. Similarly, Hilda, who ran the double monastery in Whitby at the end of her life, was a princess in the East Anglian royal family (which was closely related to the Northumbrian royal line). Bede tells us in *The Ecclesiastical History of the English People* that Hilda lived her life in two halves: the first half as a princess in the palaces, and the second as a nun and bride of Christ.

We may not have a particularly spectacular physical ancestry, but our spiritual heritage can be just as important. Those people of our past who form our spiritual ancestry can be a part of who we are, including the Celtic saints.

But as we prepare to enter the story of the birth of Christ, to contemplate the first of the three comings of Christ, let us focus on this incarnational concept of the Cosmic Christ taking on a body and stepping into an earthly family line.

Contemplation

Take the picture you had yesterday of the Chi Rho page.

This time, instead of focusing on just the illuminated letters at the top, draw your contemplations from them towards the words at the bottom of the page.

Once again, allow your imagination to feel what it may have been like for the Cosmic Christ to flow into human form from the supernatural realm. Focus this time on the humanity of Christ, on becoming small and dwelling in the womb of Mary, and growing into the next person who would be born into this ancestral line.

Think also of those of your own spiritual heritage. Who in that ancestral line inspires you?

Reading

An account of the genealogy of Jesus the Messiah, the son of David, the son of Abraham.

Abraham was the father of Isaac, and Isaac the father of Jacob, and Jacob the father of Judah and his brothers, and Judah the father of Perez and Zerah by Tamar, and Perez the father of Hezron, and Hezron the father of Aram, and Aram the father of Aminadab, and Aminadab the father of Nahshon, and Nahshon the father of Salmon, and Salmon the father of Boaz by Rahab, and Boaz the father of Obed by Ruth, and Obed the father of Jesse, and Jesse the father of King David.

And David was the father of Solomon by the wife of Uriah, and Solomon the father of Rehoboam, and Rehoboam the father of Abijah, and Abijah the father of Asaph, and Asaph the father of Jehoshaphat, and Jehoshaphat the father of Joram, and Joram the father of Uzziah, and Uzziah the father of Jotham, and Jotham the father of Ahaz, and Ahaz the father of Hezekiah, and Hezekiah the father of Manasseh, and Manasseh the father of Amos, and Amos the father of Josiah, and Josiah the father of Jechoniah and his brothers, at the time of the deportation to Babylon.

And after the deportation to Babylon: Jechoniah was the father of Salathiel, and Salathiel the father of Zerubbabel, and Zerubbabel the father of Abiud, and Abiud the father of Eliakim, and Eliakim the father of Azor, and Azor the father of

Zadok, and Zadok the father of Achim, and Achim the father of Eliud, and Eliud the father of Eleazar, and Eleazar the father of Matthan, and Matthan the father of Jacob, and Jacob the father of Joseph the husband of Mary, of whom Jesus was born, who is called the Messiah.

So all the generations from Abraham to David are fourteen generations; and from David to the deportation to Babylon, fourteen generations; and from the deportation to Babylon to the Messiah, fourteen generations.

MATTHEW 1:1–17

Prayer

Cosmic Christ, as I prepare to enter the story of your incarnation, help me to draw to mind those of my own spiritual heritage who inspire me. Thank you for the lives which have been lived for you in the past, and may I live a life of inspiration to others. Amen

The first coming of Christ

This section of the 40 days is to remember what we all focus on at Christmas time: the coming of Christ into the world as a baby, to remember the incarnation of Christ.

20 November

Today, we begin ten days of focusing on the first coming of Christ, the incarnation, the birth of Jesus, the pinnacle of the Christmas story. God becoming incarnate is a deeply significant part of the relationship which creation (including humanity) has with its Creator. The incarnation is worthy of its own focus. I have known some Christians to almost dismiss the significance of the incarnation by drawing focus away from the birth of Jesus and simply focusing on the cross, the Easter story. Although the cross is a deeply significant aspect of the life and mission of the Christ, and is intrinsic to eternal salvation, the birth is also worthy of its own specific, significant focus. Christmas, the incarnation of the Christ, is *not* about the cross; it is about the God of the whole universe, the Creator of all things, the ineffable Almighty One becoming flesh and blood and moving into our world as one of us.

So significant was the birth of Christ to the Celtic Christians that a myth arose that a fifth-century Irish saint, Brigid of Kildare, was actually transported back in time to the place where Mary and Joseph were and was the delivery midwife to Jesus himself.[6] The Celtic Christians believed (as most Christians did and still do) that God is not caught within linear time as the created universe is, therefore all of history was always happening in the eyes of the ineffable God all at once. They believed that, if God could pick someone up and transport them in *space* from one place to another (see Acts 8:39–40), then God could also pick someone up and transport them in *time* from one place to another. There is a famous painting by the Scottish artist John Duncan called 'Saint Bride' (1913) of Brigid being lifted by two angels from her own time and being taken to the birthplace (and time) of Christ. Imagine what it would be like to be in a situation like the story of Brigid.

Contemplation

As we begin our ten-day focus on the first coming of Christ, the incarnation, consider how you feel about the whole idea that the Almighty Creator of the universe, the Creator of time and existence itself, would take on flesh and become a baby.

Reading

> In the sixth month of Elizabeth's pregnancy, God sent the angel Gabriel to Nazareth, a village in Galilee, to a virgin named Mary. She was engaged to be married to a man named Joseph, a descendant of King David. Gabriel appeared to her and said, 'Greetings, favoured woman! The Lord is with you!'
>
> Confused and disturbed, Mary tried to think what the angel could mean. 'Don't be afraid, Mary,' the angel told her, 'for you have found favour with God! You will conceive and give birth to a son, and you will name him Jesus. He will be very great and will be called the Son of the Most High. The Lord God will give him the throne of his ancestor David. And he will reign over Israel forever; his Kingdom will never end!'
>
> Mary asked the angel, 'But how can this happen? I am a virgin.'
>
> The angel replied, 'The Holy Spirit will come upon you, and the power of the Most High will overshadow you. So the baby to be born will be holy, and he will be called the Son of God. What's more, your relative Elizabeth has become pregnant in her old age! People used to say she was barren, but she has conceived a son and is now in her sixth month. For the word of God will never fail.'
>
> Mary responded, 'I am the Lord's servant. May everything you have said about me come true.' And then the angel left her.
>
> LUKE 1:26–38 (NLT)

Prayer

Christ Jesus, as you grew in the womb of Mary, the incarnation began to come about. As I contemplate the significance and importance of this act, expand my understanding of your stepping out of glory, and of your willingness to step into this feeble, restricted form. Amen

21 November

For the Celts, songs, poems and epic sagas were an intrinsic part of their everyday life. They carried deep spiritual meanings and sometimes encouragement into the reality and often harshness of life. From ancient stories of such enigmatic figures as Cú Chulainn in Ireland from the pre-Christian period, to the later Welsh tales found in the *Mabinogion*, stories and hero sagas were in the Celtic blood. Bards, storytellers and singers in the pre-Christian Druidic era of the Celtic nations could hold positions as high as politicians and royal Druidic advisors. The Angles and the Saxons were just the same, with such songs as 'The Seafarer' and 'The Wanderer' being preserved so that we know them today.

This whole concept of song as part of the soul of a community was in the lifeblood of the Celtic and Anglo-Saxon peoples. And this didn't stop when Christianity became the more dominant faith. Bede tells us in his *Ecclesiastical History of the English People* that monastic centres, such as Hilda's in Whitby, maintained the cultural tradition of passing a harp round at feasts, where each would have the chance to sing or tell a tale or two of adventure, or heroes, or great spiritual encounters.[7]

One of those epic Christian hero sagas was the poem 'The Dream of the Rood'[8] depicting Christ as the Warrior Hero going to battle on the cross. We also have a tiny fragment of Cædmon's hymn of the creation of the universe, a divinely inspired song to a man who could previously not sing or even remember a song. Praise through poem and song for what God was doing and had done was ever on the lips of the Celtic saints, known to chant psalms as they walked.

Today, we continue to understand this concept of poems and song from within the Celtic culture. You cannot buy any Celtic prayer book or poetry book without finding at least a handful of contributions from the *Carmina Gadelica*. This collection of hundreds of Celtic songs and poems and incantations, which includes Christmas carols, was brought together in the late 19th century by Alexander Carmichael, who travelled around the Scottish Highlands and Islands collecting many of these from local folk who had passed them down from one generation to the next in the oral tradition. Although they cannot be classed as 'ancient' in the same way that some other songs can be, such as the words to 'Be thou my vision', which can be dated back to eighth-century Ireland, we do know that they reflect very well the ideas and concepts, and certainly the tradition of poem and song, found in ancient Celtic culture.

In Luke 1, we find Mary using this same form of expression when she is with Elizabeth. She glorifies God with a song because of who God is, what God has done within her and what God will do through her. This song, known as the Magnificat, is Mary's expression of praise to God in the way which seems, from both Hebraic and Celtic/Anglo-Saxon culture, to be a most natural way to express our innermost senses and feelings.

Contemplation

Stories and songs and poems can be so powerful. Today, in our modern culture, music and song are used to emote responses when we are watching films and programmes; our world is still so full of the music industry that you can go almost nowhere without hearing something. Songs, poems and other such creative expressions are simply a part of who we are, of who God created us to be.

When you read the Magnificat in a moment, contemplate what song is in your heart. What is the music which plays there, and what are the words which will bubble up when no one is looking?

Maybe write down or sing something to God and continue this ancient way of expressing the very depths of our being to the divine.

Reading

> In those days Mary set out and went with haste to a Judean town in the hill country, where she entered the house of Zechariah and greeted Elizabeth. When Elizabeth heard Mary's greeting, the child leaped in her womb. And Elizabeth was filled with the Holy Spirit and exclaimed with a loud cry, 'Blessed are you among women, and blessed is the fruit of your womb. And why has this happened to me, that the mother of my Lord comes to me? For as soon as I heard the sound of your greeting, the child in my womb leaped for joy. And blessed is she who believed that there would be a fulfilment of what was spoken to her by the Lord.'
>
> And Mary said,
> 'My soul magnifies the Lord,
>   and my spirit rejoices in God my Saviour,
> for he has looked with favour on the lowliness of his servant.
>   Surely, from now on all generations will call me blessed;
> for the Mighty One has done great things for me,
>   and holy is his name.
> His mercy is for those who fear him
>   from generation to generation.
> He has shown strength with his arm;
>   he has scattered the proud in the thoughts of their hearts.
> He has brought down the powerful from their thrones,
>   and lifted up the lowly;
> he has filled the hungry with good things,
>   and sent the rich away empty.
> He has helped his servant Israel,
>   in remembrance of his mercy,
> according to the promise he made to our ancestors,
>   to Abraham and to his descendants forever.'

And Mary remained with her about three months and then returned to her home.

LUKE 1:39–56

Prayer

Creator God, who places inspiration for song into the hearts and souls of your people, place in me the song of my heart. The song you wish me to sing for you, of you, to you. May it well up within me with the sound of heavenly music so that it bursts out of me and comes into being (even if it is only when no one else is around). Amen

22 November

One cold winter's morning in the seventh century in the north of England, in the city of Ripon, a lone monk readied himself to begin his work in the guest quarters of the monastery. This young monk, Cuthbert, who had been trained in Melrose, was in charge of hospitality in this new centre which had been given to the Celtic monks after the king who owned the land had been converted to Celtic Christianity. At the top of the hill (probably where the current cathedral stands), Cuthbert busied himself getting everything ready for a full day of normal monastic chores and life. The light outside was just beginning to grow, but the air remained cold from the night. The snow had fallen all night but had now stopped and the sky was clear of clouds, which meant a very cold day was coming.

As Cuthbert left his room in the inner buildings of the monastic centre and walked across the yard, he saw a young man sitting there. Startled, Cuthbert looked at the young man and thought that he must have travelled all night in the freezing conditions and snow-laden winds and come upon the monastery and decided to seek some refuge and rest. Without hesitation, Cuthbert went to the young man. He ushered the man in and made him comfortable. As the man sat in a chair, Cuthbert knelt down before him and began to wash and warm his feet with a towel. While they waited for the bakers to finish cooking the morning bread, Cuthbert prayed for the stranger and encouraged him in the divine name.

When the bread had been baked, Cuthbert set a table for the stranger. Once Cuthbert was sure his guest was comfortable, he went to get him some warm food, because if the stranger went away now he could faint from hunger before he reached his destination, which he had told Cuthbert was very far away. But when Cuthbert returned, he found the place at the table empty. Cuthbert went outside to follow the tracks that should have been left by his guest in the untouched snow so that he could catch him up, but there were none. Cuthbert was astonished at this and turned to go back into the guest house. When he re-entered, he was greeted with a most wondrous aroma. Looking around, he saw three great loaves of bread, warm and of unusual excellence. Cuthbert realised that his visitor had been an angel, and that these loaves were of heavenly making, for he said, 'They excel the lily in whiteness, the rose in fragrance, and honey in taste. Hence it follows that they have not come from this earth of ours, but they have been brought from the paradise of joy.'[9]

Following this angelic encounter, Cuthbert continued in his life with numerous other similar encounters. Bede tells us, in this same story, that Cuthbert was 'very often held worthy to see and talk with angels'.[10]

Angelic encounters were not uncommon for the Celtic saints, whether that be a physical encounter, like the story above, or a visitation in a vision or dream. In the same way, the angel Gabriel appeared to Joseph in a dream telling him that all things would be well with Mary, and that she had been especially chosen for this most remarkable role in human history: to hold the growing Messiah in her womb and then to give birth to him. Joseph was, understandably, initially greatly disturbed at finding his betrothed to be pregnant, but he believed the angelic visitation in his dream and followed the divine plan, just as Mary did.

Contemplation

What do you think of the interaction of angels with humans? Have you ever had an encounter yourself or know someone who has?

What about visions and dreams?

The Bible tells us that the angels are commanded by God to minister to us (Hebrews 1:14), and that we may encounter angels in human form (Hebrews 13:2), just as Cuthbert did in this story. But how much do we really expect that and believe it to be real?

And if something strange or unexplainable did happen, such as in the story above, would we believe that we could have just had an angelic encounter?

Do we heed dreams, like Joseph, which may be God sending angels to speak to us?

Just pause for a moment now and consider: what do you really believe about angels?

Reading

> Now the birth of Jesus the Messiah took place in this way. When his mother Mary had been engaged to Joseph, but before they lived together, she was found to be with child from the Holy Spirit. Her husband Joseph, being a righteous man and unwilling to expose her to public disgrace, planned to dismiss her quietly. But just when he had resolved to do this, an angel of the Lord appeared to him in a dream and said, 'Joseph, son of David, do not be afraid to take Mary as your wife, for the child conceived in her is from the Holy Spirit. She will bear a son, and you are to name him Jesus, for he will save his people from their sins.' All this took place to fulfil what had been spoken by the Lord through the prophet:
>
> 'Look, the virgin shall conceive and bear a son,
> and they shall name him Emmanuel,'
>
> which means, 'God is with us.' When Joseph awoke from sleep, he did as the angel of the Lord commanded him; he took her

as his wife, but had no marital relations with her until she had borne a son; and he named him Jesus.

MATTHEW 1:18–25

Prayer

Loving God, Creator of angels, thank you that you desire to guide us and protect us through angelic encounters. May we see more of them within our churches. May we become aware of when you are speaking to us through such a way. May we live a life believing that the supernatural is woven through the natural, and that we may see angels in our daily life. Amen

23 November

So many of the Celtic saints took journeys and voyages. They were known as 'peregrini'. 'Peregrini' means one who travels or wanders from place to place. It comes from the Latin *peregrinus* which means 'foreign' or 'travelling'. The Celtic saints took journeys across land and sea, both of which were hazardous in those days. They travelled between countries, leaving the mark of Christ wherever they went. In his book *Voyages of the Celtic Saints*, Graham Panes says this:

> The Celtic saints were restless, energetic, adventurous people who thrived in the rough and tumble, chaotic, often dangerous world of post-Roman Britain... Many of the saints were adventurous travellers over great distances, frequently making long sea-going voyages in small craft over dangerous seaways... They undertook such arduous voyages and exposed themselves to such constant danger.[11]

Although the Celtic saints travelled land and sea in dangerous times, they believed that they were following a divine call, and so were under the protective hand of God, as this poem attributed to Columba shows:

> *Alone with none but thee, my God,*
> *I journey on my way.*
> *What need I fear when thou art near,*
> *Oh King of night and day?*
> *More safe am I within thy hand*
> *Than if a host should round me stand.*

In the *Anglo-Saxon Chronicles*, one of the most significant historical documents of its age, there is a record of three Irish monks, Dubslane, Macbeth and Maelinmum, landing on the shores of Cornwall who desired to 'live in a state of pilgrimage, for the love of God, they recked not where'.[12] We are told that they were in a small craft (a coracle) with no sail, no oars and no rudder. They were taken to King Alfred (the Great) to explain why they had landed. They had been set out to sea by their fellow monks in Ireland with enough provisions for seven days, and believed that God would guide their craft to wherever it was supposed to go according to the divine plan. Wherever it landed, there they would begin their mission of sharing the gospel of Christ. It is assumed that this was not a one-off incident, but that this was a practice of the Celtic saints. Wherever they travelled, they believed God was with them.

In the part of the Christmas story we look at today, Mary and Joseph travel from Nazareth to Bethlehem. This too was a journey which had its dangers. Not an easy journey and one of over 60 miles across some difficult terrain. Although we don't really know much about this journey (no little donkey to carry Mary is ever mentioned in the Bible, although it is a good assumption), we do know that both of these two people had an incredible faith in God and the divine plan that had been set out to them previously. We can intelligently surmise that, just like the Celtic saints, they would have taken this journey with total faith that God was with them and that God would protect them. Words like those from the above poem could have been on their lips.

Contemplation

What sort of journeys do you take? These days, we probably don't even think of what dangers might be out there. We are unlikely to be set upon by bandits or robbers as we drive the length of the country in our cars, or when we take a boat or plane to another country, but there are still dangers.

When we set out upon a journey, do we place ourselves and our companions into the divine hands? Do we place the journey itself into the divine hands?

Spend a moment just contemplating any journey you may be about to face, short or long, perhaps to see family or friends over Christmas. Practise placing this journey into God's hands. Keep this practice in each journey you take.

Reading

> In those days a decree went out from Emperor Augustus that all the world should be registered. This was the first registration and was taken while Quirinius was governor of Syria. All went to their own towns to be registered. Joseph also went from the town of Nazareth in Galilee to Judea, to the city of David called Bethlehem, because he was descended from the house and family of David. He went to be registered with Mary, to whom he was engaged and who was expecting a child.
>
> LUKE 2:1–5

Prayer

Christ, when you were on the earth, you walked many miles, travelling from town to town, walking in wildernesses and upon mountains. Wherever I journey today, Lord, may I be aware of your presence with me. I place my travels into the divine hands and release them into the divine plan. Keep me safe, Lord, as I go from here to there, but above all, whatever happens, may I know you ever with me. Amen

24 November

Today, about a month before Christmas, we focus on the birth of Jesus. For the Christian faith, this is one of the most important, significant parts of the whole story: the incarnation of the divine. This is the moment the Jews had been awaiting for generations, and some still are – the coming to earth of the Messiah: the very centre of the Judaic and now Christian faith. But how does the Bible deal with this birth? This amazing phenomenon of God taking on a human body? By giving it one verse, well, half a verse really, as the second half of the verse is about how the baby was wrapped and where he was laid. Luke 2:7a says: 'And [Mary] gave birth to her firstborn son.' That's it! How understated. How meek. How perfect for the beginning of the servant of all who 'emptied himself, taking the form of a slave, being born in human likeness' (Philippians 2:7).

There are a vast number of life stories of Celtic saints. Some we know nothing about until they arrive in the story as adults, such as Aidan who founded Lindisfarne. But others we know about their birth, and even the pregnancy of their mother. Some of them even had a prophetic aspect to their birth, such as Hilda who founded Whitby. The prophecy of Hilda's birth was of her bringing divine light to the whole of Britain: the coming of a light which covers the land, which blocks out the darkness there. The prophecy about Hilda's birth, in this respect, reflects the birth of Jesus, the coming of the light of Christ which covers the whole world, overcoming the darkness there.

Bede records that while Breguswith, Hilda's mother, was pregnant with Hilda, Cerdic, Breguswith's husband, was in exile. During his time in exile, Cerdic was poisoned. At this time, Breguswith dreamed that Cerdic was taken from her. She began to search for him in her dream, finishing her search by looking under her dress. There she found a most precious and incredible necklace, the light and glory of which 'spread such a blaze of light that it filled all Britain with its gracious splendour. This dream was truly fulfilled in her daughter Hild[a]; for her life was an example of the works of light.'[13]

This prophecy about the birth and life of Hilda was a sign that the divine light would be with Hilda and shine through her in the life that she led. Hilda's birth itself is not mentioned, only that she lived as a princess for the first half of her life.

Contemplation

What does it say to you that the actual birth of Christ is so understated? How does this reflect the understanding that you have of Christ's teaching about humility and meekness?

The reflection of the prophecy of Hilda's birth, of her bringing light to her nation, is just one of the stories of the births of saints. In what ways do you think Hilda was an example of the works of light? How might you be more like Hilda in the way you live your life?

Reading

> While they were there, the time came for her to deliver her child. And she gave birth to her firstborn son and wrapped him in bands of cloth, and laid him in a manger, because there was no place for them in the inn.
>
> LUKE 2:6–7

Prayer

God incarnate, as you took on human form and entered the world, you did so in a quiet and unassuming way. The record of this actual moment is just one half of a Bible verse. Help me not to seek glory or recognition for the things I do for you, for the examples of the works of light I embody. May all the glory go to God, the Creator of all. Amen

25 November

One night, a group of shepherds were sitting on the hillside watching the sheep. One of their number, a young man who was not one of the shepherds but who was taking a turn watching the sheep, saw something which he did not expect. As he sat there in the dead of night, the sky began to become unnaturally light. As he looked at the light in the distance, he saw angels coming down from heaven to the earth. This young man witnessed the angels collect something of immense brightness from the earth and draw it back up into heaven, after which the light disappeared and the night returned to normal.

The young man jumped up and woke up the shepherds to tell them what had just happened. He was convinced that the bright light which he had seen the angels collect from the earth must have been the soul of some great bishop or saint who had died that night. And he was right.

Cuthbert was from a high-class family of Angles. He was probably in the military, or in training for the military, when he had this vision of angels coming down from heaven to collect the soul of Bishop Aidan of Lindisfarne on the night that Aidan died in Bamburgh.

It was the experience of this mystical vision which convinced Cuthbert to give up his family and his military training and join the monastic life. Cuthbert decided to go to the monastic centre at Melrose where, on his approach, as he got off his horse and gave his spear to his servant, the prior of the monastery, Boisil, who was standing at the gate, 'foreseeing in spirit how great the man whom he saw was going to be in his manner of life, uttered this one sentence to those standing by: "Behold the servant of the Lord!".'[14]

This vision of angels in the sky as Cuthbert was watching the sheep at night obviously partially reflects the scene we look at today in the nativity story, where the shepherds who were sitting on the hillside outside Bethlehem saw the angels appear in the sky to proclaim Jesus' birth.

These angels were different to the one whom Cuthbert encountered in the story we read a few days ago (22 November). The angel in the previous story came in the form of a human being. These, in both the story of Cuthbert and that of the Bethlehem shepherds, came as glorious angelic beings shining a divine light across the night sky. They seem to be the stereotypical angels – larger than life, bright, shining beings. The response of both the shepherds and Cuthbert was to leave what they were doing and go and seek Jesus. For Cuthbert, it was to seek a life in the monastery; for the biblical shepherds, it was to seek the newly born Messiah. Either way, they left what they were doing and set off to find Jesus.

Contemplation

Following these angelic visions, these men left what they were doing to find Jesus. One set out just literally to find the baby Jesus, but Cuthbert set out to engage in a whole life dedicated to Jesus.

What was it that caused you to find Jesus and begin to live a life for him? It may not have been anything as dramatic as an angelic vision in the night sky of shining heavenly beings, but there was probably something or even someone.

Spend a moment contemplating what or who it was, and thank God that it/they were there at the start of your journey, drawing you on to the first step of your life path with Christ.

Reading

In that region there were shepherds living in the fields, keeping watch over their flock by night. Then an angel of the Lord stood before them, and the glory of the Lord shone around them, and they were terrified. But the angel said to them, 'Do not be afraid; for see – I am bringing you good news of great joy for all the people: to you is born this day in the city of David a Saviour, who is the Messiah, the Lord. This will be a sign for you: you will find a child wrapped in bands of cloth and lying in a manger.' And suddenly there was with the angel a multitude of the heavenly host, praising God and saying,

Glory to God in the highest heaven,
and on earth peace among those whom he favours!'

When the angels had left them and gone into heaven, the shepherds said to one another, 'Let us go now to Bethlehem and see this thing that has taken place, which the Lord has made known to us.' So they went with haste and found Mary and Joseph, and the child lying in the manger. When they saw this, they made known what had been told them about this child; and all who heard it were amazed at what the shepherds told them. But Mary treasured all these words and pondered them in her heart. The shepherds returned, glorifying and praising God for all they had heard and seen, as it had been told them.

LUKE 2:8–20

Prayer

Holy, good Shepherd, as you watch over your flock, of which I am a part, I trust that you know what is best for me, and I commit to getting to know your voice better and following you, wherever you lead me. Amen

26 November

For many of the Celtic saints, and in fact many of the ancient saints from other streams in the heritage of the Christian faith, we know very little about their childhood. Most of their stories begin when they either enter the monastic centres or they begin their ministry. So, for example, the story from yesterday when Cuthbert saw the vision of the angels would usually be the start of their biography in the *Lives* which were written about them. For some of the saints, however, we have biographers and hagiographers who have written about times when they were children. And Cuthbert is one of those.

In Shakespeare's *Twelfth Night*, we find the phrase, 'Some are born great, some achieve greatness, and some have greatness thrust upon 'em.'[15] Cuthbert, it seems, was one who was born great, or at least learned of his destiny at a very early age.

In the anonymous life of Cuthbert, the writer tells us this:

> When [Cuthbert] was a boy of eight years he surpassed all of his age in agility and high spirits, so that often after the others had gone to rest their weary limbs, he, standing triumphantly in the playground as though he were in an arena, would still wait for someone to play with him.[16]

One day around this same time, Cuthbert was with a group of children doing all sorts of different games and athletic competitions with each other. The anonymous monk tells us that among this group of children with Cuthbert 'was a certain child scarcely three years old who began to call out to him repeatedly "be steadfast and leave this foolish play". Seeing his commands disregarded [the child] wailed and wept and became almost inconsolable.' When the child was calmed down and asked what he was talking about he said, 'O holy bishop and priest Cuthbert, these unnatural tricks done to show off your agility are not befitting to you or your high office.'[17]

Although Cuthbert did not clearly understand what was being said (only being eight years old at the time), we are told by the author that Cuthbert then returned home to contemplate this prophetic cry. We know that as Cuthbert grew he had more encounters with the supernatural and experiences of God, until that time in his late teens or early 20s when he was on the hillside with the shepherds.

It can be hard for those who are 'born great', as there can sometimes be an unhelpful amount of pressure placed upon them. But this doesn't change the fact that, as Shakespeare so rightly said, some are, indeed, born great. Their divine destiny is open before them from a very early age, and they live a life fulfilling that destiny.

Contemplation

What do you believe about your destiny? Do you believe that God has a divine plan which is unfolding before you as you walk the path of life?

If this is what is happening throughout human history, what part do you have to plan in your own unfolding destiny?

If you were told something in a prophetic way, like Cuthbert was, would you go away and contemplate these things?

Spend some time with God now just contemplating the unfolding of your life path, how it has been and perhaps anything which you have been told about its future.

Reading

After eight days had passed, it was time to circumcise the child; and he was called Jesus, the name given by the angel before he was conceived in the womb.

When the time came for their purification according to the law of Moses, they brought him up to Jerusalem to present him to the Lord (as it is written in the law of the Lord, 'Every firstborn male shall be designated as holy to the Lord'), and they offered a sacrifice according to what is stated in the law of the Lord, 'a pair of turtle-doves or two young pigeons.'

Now there was a man in Jerusalem whose name was Simeon; this man was righteous and devout, looking forward to the consolation of Israel, and the Holy Spirit rested on him. It had been revealed to him by the Holy Spirit that he would not see death before he had seen the Lord's Messiah. Guided by the Spirit, Simeon came into the temple; and when the parents brought in the child Jesus, to do for him what was customary under the law, Simeon took him in his arms and praised God, saying,

'Master, now you are dismissing your servant in peace,
according to your word;
for my eyes have seen your salvation,
which you have prepared in the presence of all peoples,
a light for revelation to the Gentiles
and for glory to your people Israel.'

And the child's father and mother were amazed at what was being said about him. Then Simeon blessed them and said to his mother Mary, 'This child is destined for the falling and the rising of many in Israel, and to be a sign that will be opposed so that the inner thoughts of many will be revealed—and a sword will pierce your own soul too.'

There was also a prophet, Anna the daughter of Phanuel, of the tribe of Asher. She was of a great age, having lived with her

husband seven years after her marriage, then as a widow to the age of eighty-four. She never left the temple but worshiped there with fasting and prayer night and day. At that moment she came, and began to praise God and to speak about the child to all who were looking for the redemption of Jerusalem.
LUKE 2:21–38

Prayer

Great and loving God, thank you for the care you place on my life from the moment my existence begins. Thank you for the care that you give as my life unfolds day by day. May I know your presence with me as I walk this path of life, and may I know your word spoken into my life by others to help me along this path. Amen

27 November

Now we come to one of the most fascinating parts of the nativity story. We saw yesterday that there were two wise prophets, Anna and Simeon, from the Hebrew faith, conveniently placed near where Jesus was born to make statements about Jesus as the Messiah. However, God also decided to send magi from the east, who had discerned the birth of the Christ through interpreting the movement of the stars, to visit Jesus and make prophetic proclamations about him through the gifts that they brought.

We can discern from some sections of the Jewish *Talmud* that the Jews understood 'magi' to be Zoroastrian priests from Persia, roughly modern-day Iraq and Iran, east of the Holy Land.[18]

The term 'magi' is also used in some of the *Lives* of the Celtic saints when referring to the Druids. For example, Columba had travelled from Iona to the furthest northern-most end of Loch Ness to take the gospel to the stronghold of King Brude. As he and those with him began to sing spiritual songs for Vespers, 'certain Magi [Druids] approaching them did everything they could to prevent the sound of divine praise'.[19] In his notes to this passage, Wentworth Huyshe states that 'the word "Magi" is always used in the acts of the Irish Saints to mean the Druids'.[20]

Kenneth R. McIntosh notes that the historian Muirchú, who wrote the (earliest known) life of St Patrick, also refers to magi. In the section when King Lóegaire met Patrick, he notes that Lóegaire was not surprised at Patrick's arrival 'because *magi* had advised him of Patrick's coming'. He goes on to say that 'Muirchú used the word *magi* to show God at work in his Druid ancestors'.[21]

In his explanation of Muirchú's life of Patrick in *Celtic Theology*, Thomas O'Loughlin suggests that Muirchú uses the same term as the Bible uses to bring a connection between the two stories, and also to show that the Christian mission of Patrick to Ireland was 'not a case of Christianity walking into a void into a place where God is not, where religion is not, culture is not – nor into a place where the Spirit has not been at work'[22] – but that God was at work in Ireland already. It seems, perhaps, like Matthew when he wrote his gospel, that early Irish writers suggested that God was at work through those who others may not class as 'Christians', or God-fearing men. In the passage about the magi, the gospel writer seems to strongly suggest that God can, and does, speak through those who are from other faiths.

Contemplation

Who do you believe that God can work in and through? Do you believe that God only works in and through those who believe like you do? Or even just those who call themselves 'Christian'? Or can God work in and through anyone, no matter what they believe, or even if they say they believe nothing?

If someone from a faith outside Christianity came to you saying God sent them or gave them a word for you, would you listen?

Reading

> In the time of King Herod, after Jesus was born in Bethlehem of Judea, wise men from the East came to Jerusalem, asking, 'Where is the child who has been born king of the Jews? For we observed his star at its rising, and have come to pay him homage.' When King Herod heard this, he was frightened, and all Jerusalem with him; and calling together all the chief priests and scribes of the people, he inquired of them where

the Messiah was to be born. They told him, 'In Bethlehem of Judea; for so it has been written by the prophet:

"And you, Bethlehem, in the land of Judah,
 are by no means least among the rulers of Judah;
for from you shall come a ruler
 who is to shepherd my people Israel."'

Then Herod secretly called for the wise men and learned from them the exact time when the star had appeared. Then he sent them to Bethlehem, saying, 'Go and search diligently for the child; and when you have found him, bring me word so that I may also go and pay him homage.' When they had heard the king, they set out; and there, ahead of them, went the star that they had seen at its rising, until it stopped over the place where the child was. When they saw that the star had stopped, they were overwhelmed with joy. On entering the house, they saw the child with Mary his mother; and they knelt down and paid him homage. Then, opening their treasure chests, they offered him gifts of gold, frankincense, and myrrh. And having been warned in a dream not to return to Herod, they left for their own country by another road.

MATTHEW 2:1–12

Prayer

I thank you that you are an unlimited God, a God who is not bound by the limitations of human understanding. You are a God who loves and works in all life, whether or not they acknowledge you and who you are. May I be willing to see and hear you, knowing your voice, wherever it comes from and whomever you choose to speak through. Amen

28 November

Matthew and Luke are the two gospel writers who tell the nativity story. The whole of this story, all the plays in school and all the films – all of what we have looked at so far in the section on the first coming of Christ – come from the accounts found in Matthew and Luke. Mark begins his gospel not at the birth of Jesus, but at the start of his adult ministry. John, however, begins somewhere quite different. John, who many view as a mystical writer, begins his gospel with the theology of the Cosmic Christ: that is, although the incarnation happened at a particular moment in time in human history, the Christ has always existed.

In the ninth century, an Irish mystic theologian who had great influence across the whole of Europe wrote a homily on the beginning of John's gospel, on John's account of the Cosmic Christ becoming incarnate. John Scotus Eriugena wrote this homily about the incarnation of Christ and what that means for us now. In the chapter entitled 'The Word made flesh', Eriugena says:

> If the Son of God is made a human being, which none of those who receive him doubt... indeed, the Word descended into the flesh... [then] the human being, believing through the flesh in the Word, might ascend; that through him who was the only begotten Son by nature, many might become sons by adoption.[23]

Eriugena suggests that we can become children of God, that is, to take on the divine essence and nature, because Christ took on our humanity – became flesh. We can become God's children because the only begotten Son became human.

In the same section, Eriugena goes on to say:

> He who from God made himself a human being, makes gods from human beings. [Scripture says] 'and dwelt among us' – that is, possessed our nature so as to make us participants in his nature.[24]

That is to say, Christ gave up his divine glory and took on humanity so that we might transcend our humanity to put on his divine nature. By this, we are able to become children of God, adopted into the divine family, so that we can become one with God.

Contemplation

What does it mean to become one with God – to take on the divine essence and nature?

For Eriugena, the reason Christ became incarnate was so that all things could be reconciled with the divine and so that we can become one with God now, and take on the divine nature in this world, as we live day by day. It wasn't just about what happens to us after we die, but what we allow God to do within us while we live.

Spend time with God, with Christ, dwelling on how you might better become one with the divine and take on the divine nature in the life you live day by day.

Reading

In the beginning was the Word, and the Word was with God, and the Word was God… To all who received him, who believed in his name, he gave power to become children of God, who were born, not of blood or of the will of the flesh or of the will of man, but of God. And the Word became flesh and lived among us, and we have seen his glory, the glory as of a father's only son, full of grace and truth.

JOHN 1:1–2, 12–14

Prayer

Christ, you stepped out of transcendent glory and took on human form so that I might transcend my humanity and be clothed in the divine nature. Help me to see this and to walk this path of becoming more and more like you as you transform me from one degree of glory to the next. Amen

29 November

In Christopher Bamford's reflections of John Scotus Eriugena's homily on the prologue of John's gospel, he says:

> At the time of the Incarnation of the Word, the world lay shrouded in darkness. Following it, the world – though illuminated now by the Light – still labours in the delusion and obscurity of a sense world apparently cut off from the light of true knowledge, the world of meaning. But this duality is now illusory, for the Light has shone, and the way to unity has been reopened.[25]

For Bamford, the way into the unity with the divine, as described by Eriugena in his homily, is open to us. The fact that we live our lives as if the Word had not come, and as if we are still in the prison of darkness rather than the freedom of the Light, is an illusion, one which can be overcome.[26] This living in the awareness of the Light is a choice we make of allowing that Light to shine within us. Bamford says:

> This is a real rising up of the sense perceptible into the spiritual. Sin, death, suffering – all the paraphernalia of the prince of the world – are overcome. The world dwells in the light. Suddenly the veil of phenomenal reality is punctuated and permeated by God's transcendent Word, his presence.[27]

Our world, our lives, are punctuated and permeated by the divine presence. We need to live in the reality of this, rather than the illusion that the world, our inner world, is still in darkness. We need not feel like we are abandoned by God in a world of darkness but, as Bamford continues to say:

> The Word which spoke from without now speaks from within. A new age dawns... No longer need we feel abandoned and destitute in a material world of fragmentation and disunion... For us, post-Incarnation human beings, this process [of transformation] has already begun.[28]

We can live our lives in the process of this divine transformation. This does not mean that we will not encounter the darkness that still exists in the world, but part of being in the world but not of it means that, as the apostle Paul says, we may be 'afflicted in every way, but not crushed; perplexed, but not driven to despair; persecuted, but not forsaken; struck down, but not destroyed' (2 Corinthians 4:8–9). This leads us on into the next section of our contemplations: the second period of the 40 days which the Celtic Christians dwelt in, the focusing upon the second of the three comings of Christ. Over the past ten days, we have looked at the first coming, the incarnation of the Cosmic Christ into human form, that which the celebration of Christmas is all about. Now, in the next ten days, we move on to the second coming of Christ; that is, Christ coming into our lives, and how we are transformed by that.

Contemplation

What does it mean to be in the world but not of it; to be 'afflicted in every way, but not crushed; perplexed, but not driven to despair; persecuted, but not forsaken; struck down, but not destroyed'?

What can you do to begin, or continue, to live in the awareness of the reality that the Word has been made flesh, and that the Light has come into the world?

Reading

In him was life, and the life was the light of all people. The light shines in the darkness, and the darkness did not overcome it... The true light, which enlightens everyone, was coming into the world. He was in the world, and the world came into being through him; yet the world did not know him. He came to what was his own, and his own people did not accept him.

JOHN 1:4–5, 9–11

Prayer

Great Light, who shines in the depths of all darkness, may I know you in my life today. May I be aware of your Light shining in my darkness. May I live a life in the reality of what it means that you have come and overcome the darkness, rather than in the illusion of the darkness still having dominion. Amen

The second coming of Christ

This section of the 40 days is to remember the coming of Christ into our lives. For the Celtic Christians, this was not just a one-off event at the moment of conversion, but a continual need in our everyday lives.

30 November

Because of numerous prophecies in the Tanakh (the Old Testament of the Christian Bible), many Jewish people were looking for the messiah to come like a great warrior and defeat whatever system might have been imposing itself on the Israelite people at the time of his arrival. They were expecting him to be a great king in the way that their greatest historical king, David, was. This is one reason why many of the Jewish people did not recognise Jesus as the messiah. If Jesus was the messiah, he should have come in like a warrior king freeing the Holy Land from the hands of the Roman Empire. But, when questioned about his kingdom, Jesus replied that his was a different kind of kingdom. He wasn't a military leader in the worldly sense, but a warrior king whose kingdom is within his people. As he said when questioned about it, 'The kingdom of God is within you' (Luke 17:21). The word translated as 'within' in Greek is the word *entos* which means 'inside', 'in the midst' or 'within your soul'.[29] This is one place where Christ's kingdom is – dwelling within the heart and soul of the believer.

There were numerous Celtic saints who knew this difference – who were destined for military service but who decided to take up the battle of this different kingdom instead. Cadoc was one such man. He was the son of Prince Gwynllyw ap Glywys of Glywysing in Wales. He was brought up in the ways of the warrior class, learning the ways of military strategy. When he came of age, however, Cadoc refused to lead his father's men when he gained the right to do so. An Irish monk named Tathan gave Cadoc his early education in the monastic life. Cadoc learned of the spiritual battle and put the understanding of his military upbringing into that instead of physical wars. After a time of training in Ireland, Cadoc became a hermit and lived in the

Welsh mountains. One day, a band of soldiers came upon him and began to treat him terribly. Their commander, a man named Illtyd, responded like this:

> [Illtyd] was so horrified by the behaviour of the knights, but so taken by the response of the hermit, Cadoc. Cadoc refused to retaliate but simply smiled calmly and allowed the knights to carry on. Illtyd jumped from his horse and dismissed the knights and sent them away. Illtyd, though, fell to his knees before Cadoc and asked him to forgive the knights. Cadoc lifted Illtyd gently and spoke to him about a different kind of fighting, for a different King. Cadoc spoke of the kingdom of heaven and Christ the King, and of being a warrior peacemaker in the spiritual realms.
>
> That night Illtyd lay awake thinking about the words of Cadoc and of being a soldier of Christ… and of his stories of overcoming Satan. When he finally fell asleep an angel appeared to him in a dream. The angel said, 'Until now you have been a knight serving mortal kings. From now on you are to be in the service of the King of Kings.' At dawn Illtyd left the royal palace leaving his sword and armour, the sign of his service, behind him to be a soldier of Christ… He started off learning from Cadoc, and then went on to found influential centres [in Wales].[30]

Contemplation

What does it mean to you to know that the kingdom of God is within your inner being? That Christ the King is reigning in this kingdom within you?

What would it mean to truly live from within this kingdom? To truly believe that this kingdom is reigning within your inner being?

Reading

Now when He was asked by the Pharisees when the kingdom of God would come, He answered them and said, 'The kingdom of God does not come with observation; nor will they say, "See here!" or "See there!" For indeed, the kingdom of God is within you.'

LUKE 17:20–21 (NKJV)

Prayer

Christ the King, I simply say: your kingdom come within me; your will be done within me. Amen

1 December

We all know the difficulty, when we are trying to live holy lives, of the internal battle between that which we know is holy and righteous, and that which our selfish ego desires. The important thing, as we can see in numerous passages in scripture, is to continue to live out of our holiness which comes through Christ living in us, rather than gratifying the sinful desires which so often raise their heads. The Bible often refers to these two things as 'the flesh' – that is, the sinful desires of the self-centred ego which draw us away from God – and 'the spirit' – that is, the work of God to transform us more and more into the divine image which dwells within each person.

There are numerous people (we may be able to call some to mind) who use the term 'Christian' to describe themselves, but actually do not live lives which reflect that statement. They seem to live more from the flesh than from the Spirit. It is not what we call ourselves which makes the difference, but whether the Spirit of God dwells within you, whether Christ himself is in your life and from which of these two things we live.

In the seventh century, there was a large monastic centre in northern Britain in a place called Coldingham. Those who entered this place did so, as any who entered monastic centres did, to live holy lives. However, the story of the centre at Coldingham seems to show that many of those who lived there, both men and women who had taken vows and the habit, lived mostly from the flesh and not from the Spirit. The centre, Bede tells us, had become a place where the women who had taken vows to be brides of Christ were creating beautiful clothes in order to attract men and 'make friends with' (a euphemism!) men who were strangers and passers-by.[31] It seems that the monastery in Coldingham had become extremely promiscuous and those who lived there were more interested in fleshly pleasure than holy living. There is one story of St Cuthbert visiting Coldingham where he went and spent the night in the cold of the North Sea, praying. It is suggested in some modern tourist information sources that the reason Cuthbert did this was to 'cool himself off' from the sexual temptations of that place: the equivalent of the advice to someone today to 'take a cold shower'! Although I'm not convinced, I rather think he did this with the intention of increasing the holiness rather than dampening the fleshiness.

Æbbe, who was the head of this monastic centre, seemed to be unaware of what was going on as the women were doing this in secret, and Æbbe herself continued to live a holy life. It wasn't until a monk named Adamnan, who had had a prophetic vision about the monastery, went around room to room inspecting what was going on that Æbbe discovered the depth of the 'flesh life' that was being lived out in her monastery. Once Æbbe was aware, however, Bede tells us that the behaviour stopped. But only until Æbbe died, and then 'they returned to their old defilement and committed even worse crimes'.[32]

Contemplation

If Christ lives in us, then, the Bible tells us, we should not be living from the fleshly desires. This doesn't mean that they won't be there, just that we don't live from them.

How do these desires manifest within you and in your life? How do you deal with them?

Spend time with God now confessing any of these influences which have hindered your spiritual growth, but also asking that the power of Christ in you, and the work of the Spirit in you, will continue to overpower these fleshly desires and lead you into more righteous living.

Reading

Those who are in the flesh cannot please God. But you are not in the flesh; you are in the Spirit, since the Spirit of God dwells in you. Anyone who does not have the Spirit of Christ does not belong to him. But if Christ is in you, though the body is dead because of sin, the Spirit is life because of righteousness.

ROMANS 8:8–10

Prayer

Holy God, make me holy. May my flesh-life melt away. May Christ in me lead me into righteous living. Amen

2 December

In the stories in the Bible, we see instances of people being raised from the dead. This is resurrection power at work in the world in the days of the living. Resurrection power isn't just about raising your soul into a new body at the end of all time; it is about that power being at work in the world today, in our mortal bodies. This resurrection power comes from Christ within us, Christ who was raised from the dead living inside us. This was something which the Celtic saints seemed to take as a literal teaching, believing that, through the power of the risen Christ living in them, they could raise people from the dead.

One example of this comes from the life of Samson. Samson was trained under Illtyd in Wales and travelled around there, Cornwall, the Channel Islands and Brittany, which is where he concluded his ministry, and so is usually known as Samson of Dol (in Brittany). However, this story comes from one of his travels through Cornwall.

Samson was travelling through a region in Cornwall with some other monks when they saw a group of locals putting on a play about their pagan gods at a sacred place by an idol/standing stone at the top of a hill. Samson took a couple of monks with him to beseech them to stop and to tell them about Christ. While they were speaking, some of the locals getting quite angry, a young boy who was driving a team of horses at great speed rode through the gathering. As he passed through the people, the horse which he was sitting on was startled and threw him. He fell awkwardly and, as he landed, broke his neck and 'remained just as he was flung, little else than a lifeless corpse'.[33] Samson took this as an opportunity to show everyone there the resurrection power which flowed through him due to Christ dwelling within him. He challenged them to believe in his God and the Christ if he proved to them this resurrection power. 'You see your idol is not able to give aid to the dead man,' he said to them. 'Well, if you destroy your idol and turn to Christ, I will show you the power of Christ and bring the dead man back to life.'

Samson then prayed over the body of this young man for two hours. Often, we give up on our prayers, thinking that God is not going to do anything, but Samson stayed with the dead body, praying for the resurrection power of Christ to move in this mortal body before him. After two hours of prayer, Samson finally 'delivered him, who had been dead, alive and sound before them all. Seeing this they all with one accord, along with [their] chief, prostrated themselves at Samson's feet and destroyed the idol.'[34]

Contemplation

Christ rose from the dead and dwells within you with this power.

What does that mean to you? How can living in this knowledge affect the way in which you live your life day to day? How does knowing that 'he who raised Christ from the dead will give life to your mortal bodies' affect you on a daily basis?

Reading

> If the Spirit of him who raised Jesus from the dead dwells in you, he who raised Christ from the dead will give life to your mortal bodies also through his Spirit that dwells in you.
> ROMANS 8:11

Prayer

Risen Christ, living within me, may I know the power of your life moving through me. May the resurrection power, which raised you from the dead, raise me from the death which can so often take over my soul. Not only this, but may I know that power flowing through me in the days of my living. Amen

3 December

Our reading today from Ephesians speaks of strength in our inner being through Christ dwelling in our hearts and the power of the Spirit working in us. This idea of a strength in and for our inner being with Christ in us – or, more specifically, the strength of the protection of Christ – can be found in the prayers from the Celtic tradition known as the 'Lorica' or 'Breastplate' prayers. The most famous of these, arguably, is Patrick's breastplate prayer.

Patrick's breastplate prayer begins with statements of binding to one's self such things as the strong name of the Trinity; the power of faith in Christ's incarnation and various other sections of Christ's life; the power of different types of angels and some aspects of the natural creation. There is a sense of protection in one stanza against such things as the snares of demons, natural lust, Satan's spells and wiles, and wizards' evil craft.

The verse, however, which sits as the key point of this prayer is the one which states that Christ is within us and in every other surrounding area of us and our life.

> Christ be with me, Christ within me,
> Christ behind me, Christ before me,
> Christ beside me, Christ to win me,
> Christ to comfort and restore me,
> Christ beneath me, Christ above me,
> Christ in quiet, Christ in danger,
> Christ in hearts of all that love me,
> Christ in mouth of friend and stranger.[35]

The strength and grounding these lorica or breastplate prayers brought the Celtic saints, and the focus centring around the awareness of the presence of Christ not just near us but within us, shows that the coming of Christ into our lives was central to the everyday lives of the Celtic saints. At the centre of this was the belief that the power of God, dwelling in the presence of Christ in us, was greater than any of the other things mentioned and listed in these prayers, and that Christ's presence within us protected us.

Contemplation

Reread the 'Christ within me' stanza. What does it mean to you to have Christ with and within you in such a way? How does this help you become strengthened and feel protected in your everyday life?

Reading

> I pray that, according to the riches of his glory, he may grant that you may be strengthened in your inner being with power through his Spirit, and that Christ may dwell in your hearts through faith, as you are being rooted and grounded in love.
> EPHESIANS 3:16–17

Prayer

I bind unto myself today the strong name of the Trinity, by invocation of the same, the Three in One, the One in Three.

I bind this day to me forever, by power of faith, Christ's incarnation, his baptism in the Jordan river, his death on cross for my salvation; his bursting from the spiced tomb, his riding up the heavenly way, his coming at the day of doom, I bind unto myself today.[36]

4 December

Mystery is something which many in today's western culture find difficult to live with. One of the downsides of living in a 'post-Enlightenment' culture and in a scientific age is that we are conditioned in our learning to require proof. Mystery is something we are not used to living with. We don't like not knowing. For the Celtic Christians, mystery wasn't a problem; but then there seemed to be less mystery for them than for the modern Christian, as God was there in every part and aspect of life. There was no separation in the mind of the Celtic Christian between sacred and secular, between spiritual and physical. For them, everything was spiritual and God was in everything.

One of the prayers in the *Carmina Gadelica* shows this concept of God in everything. The 'God's Aid' prayer draws a deliberate sense of the divine presence into everything. It says

> God to enfold me, God to surround me, God in my speaking, God in my thinking.
> God in my sleeping, God in my waking. God in my watching, God in my hoping.
> God in my life, God in my lips, God in my hands, God in my heart.
> God in my sufficing, God in my slumber, God in mine ever-living soul, God in mine eternity.[37]

This poem/prayer from well over 100 years ago, reflecting a much more ancient understanding, is itself reflected in the lyrics of a modern song on the album 'Everything' by the contemporary Christian song writer Tim Hughes. In this song, the lyrics say:

God in my living, there in my breathing, God in my waking, God in my sleeping
God in my resting, there in my working, God in my thinking, God in my speaking
Be my everything...
God in my hoping, there in my dreaming, God in my watching, God in my waiting
God in my laughing, there in my weeping, God in my hurting, God in my healing.[38]

The lyrics in the same song then go on to say: 'Christ in me, Christ in me, Christ in me the hope of glory, You are everything.' Using wording reminiscent of the breastplate prayers we looked at yesterday, this brings a sense of the two together: the mystery of God being active and present in every part of our lives is related to the fact that Christ is in us, and that presence of Christ in us is our hope of glory.

Contemplation

How do you cope with the mysteries of the divine, the aspects which you just cannot fathom? Do they sit comfortably with you, or do you strive to have all the answers?

What do you think of the idea that God is in everything you do? We know in theory that God is everywhere, but do we live in the conscious awareness that God is in our waking, in our sleeping, in our walking, in everything?

Reading

The mystery that has been hidden throughout the ages and generations... has now been revealed to his saints. To them God chose to make known how great among the Gentiles are the riches of the glory of this mystery, which is Christ in you, the hope of glory.

COLOSSIANS 1:26–27

Prayer

Mysterious, unfathomable God, may I live in the awareness of your presence every day. As I go about my every day, may I know the presence of Christ in me, my hope of glory. Amen

5 December

The following is an edited version of the extra Celtic saint added to the Welsh translation of the book *40 Days with the Celtic Saints*.[39]

Dwynwen (or Dwyn Wen) was born into a royal household. She was the beautiful daughter of Brychan, King of Brecknock (Brecon). We know very little of her life, but she has, in recent years, had a revitalisation of being the patron saint of Welsh lovers, which she was in generations past, because of one particular story which has come down from her life.

Dwynwen was a holy woman highly dedicated to God. Her holiness was proven, legend says, by the fact that she once walked on the water to get from Wales to Ireland. However, although Dwynwen was dedicated to God, she also fell deeply in love with a man, Maelon Dafodrill, who also fell madly in love with her. The two were besotted with each other, and so naturally Maelon made advances towards Dwynwen and tried to win her. But Dwynwen, despite her desire and heartfelt love for Maelon, feeling that her dedication to God would be compromised if she responded, spurned these affectionate actions and proclamations.

Maelon became hurt and angry and his passion shifted from love to rage. The story says that he attacked Dwynwen, perhaps physically; other reports say that he simply 'cast [bad] reflections on her good name, causing her extreme sorrow and anguish'.[40]

Because of Maelon's hurtful actions, he was turned into a block of ice by drinking a potion he was given by angels. Dwynwen, meanwhile, had run deep into a forest pining in anguish at this heartache and torture. In her desperation and heartbreak, she cried out to God for help. As she prayed, two angels appeared to her, also with a potion. Upon drinking the potion, her prayers were answered, and she was cured of the heartache and of her desperate love for Maelon. God then gave Dwynwen the chance to ask three requests of anything she wanted. Her first request was that Maelon was freed from his frozen state; her second request was that she could live her life happily, chaste and without want of another; and her third and final request was that she could intercede before God for all lovelorn lovers for all time. The whole host of heaven agreed to her requests, and so God granted them.

Dwynwen lived out the rest of her life as a nun and was well known for giving advice to lovers. She spent her last years on a small islet off the coast of Anglesey where she gave her name to a church at Llanddwyn.

Of course, love is so much more, so much deeper than just the romantic, erotic love of this story. There are other aspects of love, and God is the whole spectrum of love. If we abide in this spectrum of love, God abides in us.

Contemplation

What does 'love' mean to you? When Jesus told his disciples to love one another like he had loved them, what do you think he meant?

What about romantic love? How does that fit in with your relationship with God? If you have a lover/partner, in what way does your relationship with them interweave with your faith and relationship with God?

Reading

So we have known and believe the love that God has for us.
God is love, and those who abide in love abide in God, and God abides in them.

1 JOHN 4:16

Prayer

God of love, God who is love, may I abide in the whole spectrum of love so that you would abide in me, and so that love would abide in me. Amen

6 December

For the Celtic Christians, the connection we have with God can be directly related to the connection we have with the natural world around us. They didn't just use the natural world as a metaphor or as symbolism, but they actually connected with God through it, saw God in it and were one with God within it. They fully understood the separation of the presence of God within creation and the creation itself, but they understood the creation to be an expression of the divine. When we dwell in the divine, when we are led by the Spirit, we bear the fruit of the Spirit: that is, love, joy, peace, patience, kindness, generosity, faithfulness, gentleness and self-control (Galatians 5:22–23). When we follow the will of God, we dwell in the divine and we produce this fruit.

A catechism which is attributed to the fourth-century Celtic monk Ninian says this:

> **Question**: What is best in the world?
> **Answer**: To do the will of the Maker.
>
> **Question**: What is that will?
> **Answer**: That we should live according to the laws of creation.
>
> **Question**: How do we know those laws?
> **Answer**: By study.
>
> **Question**: What tool has the Maker provided for this study?
> **Answer**: The intellect.

> **Question**: And what is the fruit of study?
> **Answer**: To perceive the eternal word of God reflected in every plant and insect, every bird and animal, and every man and woman.[41]

The connection for the Celtic Christians between doing the will of the Maker and seeing the Maker in everything which exists around us is clearly seen in this catechism, as well as in numerous other places. We live connected to the divine; we bear fruit by following the will of God; we know the will of God by studying with our intellect; the fruit, the end, the conclusion of this study is to perceive the divine in the natural world around us; by seeing the divine in everything around us, we begin to live a life of love, joy, peace, patience, kindness, generosity, faithfulness, gentleness and self-control, the fruit of the Spirit.

It is by a cycle of connection and flow that the branch of a plant produces fruit; it is part of the plant and remains connected to it; by this connection, it produces fruit. For the Celtic Christians, this was a cycle that simply continued within them and their relationship with God, with Christ. It continued to go round and round and round... Connection, divine flow, producing fruit, connection, divine flow, producing fruit...

Contemplation

How do you view and understand the natural world around you? Do you see God in it?

Does that make a difference to how you react and respond in life?

If you understood and saw God in the natural world, how might you treat it differently? Are you part of the natural, never-ending cycle and flow of connection, divine flow, producing fruit, connection, divine flow, producing fruit...?

Reading

Abide in me as I abide in you. Just as the branch cannot bear fruit by itself unless it abides in the vine, neither can you unless you abide in me. I am the vine, you are the branches. Those who abide in me and I in them bear much fruit, because apart from me you can do nothing.

JOHN 15:4–5

Prayer

Great Creator of all life, may I see you in all things, may I 'take a long and thoughtful look at what you have created, and see what my eyes can't see: your eternal power, for instance, and the mystery of your divine being'.[42] In my continued connection with you, may I bear the fruit of the Spirit, and live a life of love, joy, peace, patience, kindness, generosity, faithfulness, gentleness and self-control. Amen

7 December

The Eucharist has always been a central part of the Christian faith. This aspect of the Passover meal which Christ tells his followers to repeat is shaped by the coming of the Christ – the *matzah* which represented the body of the messiah in the Passover meal now represents the body of Jesus, the Christ; the cup of redemption which represented the blood of the sacrificial lamb now represents his blood which was shed on the cross. For the Celtic Christians, the Eucharist stood as a central part of their faith, just as it does to Christians today and has throughout the whole of Christian history. It is the act of the death and resurrection of Christ that enables us to become one with God. It is through this cosmic act that we are able to have Christ dwell in us and us in him.

There are not many parts of the actual services that the Celtic church practised which have come down to us, but one thing which has is part of a liturgy. An eighth-century liturgical text known as the Stowe Missal comes from Tallaght, Ireland.[43] This text contains instructions on conducting the Eucharist, responsive liturgy and hymns.

The Communion Hymn from the Stowe Missal says:

> Come, you holy ones, receive the body of Christ, drinking the holy blood by which you were redeemed.
> You who were saved by the body and blood of Christ, let us praise God by whom we are made anew.
> By this sacrament of the body and blood, all have escaped from the jaws of hell.
> Giver of salvation, Christ, the Son of God, has saved the world by his cross and blood.

> The Lord has been sacrificed for all, himself both priest and victim…
> Let all draw near with pure and faithful minds, let all receive the protection of eternal salvation.
> Guardian of the saints, you are leader O Lord, and dispenser of life eternal to those who believe…
> Christ the Lord himself comes, the Alpha and Omega. He shall come again to judge us all.[44]

Contemplation

'Let all draw near with pure and faithful minds.' As we draw near to God through the celebration of the Eucharist, we live in the truth of the words of scripture below that those who partake in this abide in Christ and Christ abides in them. What does this mean to you? What does the Eucharist mean to you?

Reading

> For my flesh is true food and my blood is true drink. Those who eat my flesh and drink my blood abide in me, and I in them. Just as the living Father sent me, and I live because of the Father, so whoever eats me will live because of me.
>
> JOHN 6:55–57

Prayer

As we draw near to the place of at-one-ment: give us tears to see the wonder of your presence, give us tears to see the wasting of your land, give us tears to see the wounding of your Son.[45]

8 December

The Bible tells us that those who follow the commands of Christ abide in Christ and Christ abides in them. Following the commands of Christ means more than just using his name as a religious title or identification; it means truly living a life like Christ. In the late fourth and early fifth centuries, a British monk, best known by his Latin name Pelagius, travelled from Britain to Rome. Pelagius went down in history because of his challenge to Augustine of Hippo about various aspects of theology which the British (Celtic) church felt were unbiblical and ungodly. What most people don't realise, though, is that Pelagius, before he challenged Augustine's theology, spent around 30 years in Rome as a well-respected theologian.

> Pelagius was the spiritual advisor to many Christians in Rome, and in fact moved about successfully in the Roman Christian circles of Jerome. In Rome Pelagius emerged as a theologian to be reckoned with and as a man who had great personal sanctity, moral fervour and charisma… Pelagius was evidently a major religious intellectual force of his time. He always made a point of showing that his ideas had a solid basis in the writings of the Church Fathers. At least until 415 Pelagius was widely accepted as an orthodox Christian theologian.[46]

Pelagius also wrote apostolic letters. In one of these letters is found a section called 'On the Christian life', in which he wrote:

> And let us not flatter ourselves merely on possessing the name and being *called* Christians… Who is so mad and senseless as to declare himself to be a soldier, when he does not know how to wield arms? No one is assigned any name whatever without

due course: to be called a cobbler it is necessary to produce shoes; it is his skill in his craft which causes a man to be called an artificer or craftsman... For it is by examples of this kind that we recognise that there is no name without an act but that every name comes from an act.

How can you then be called Christian, if there is no Christian act in you?... He is a Christian who is one not only in name, but in deed, who imitates and follows Christ in everything.[47]

It is from the sacrament of anointing, both of Christ and of all Christians... that the name and term [Christian] have come, which name those people have been wrongly given who imitate Christ hardly at all. How can you be called something which you are not, and falsely take another's name? But if you wish to be a Christian, then do those things that are of Christ and worthily bear the name of Christian... Perhaps you do not wish to *be* a Christian but only to be called one? Wanting to be something without actually being it is both base and wretched... Such people are not Christ's servants at all, but rather they mock and deride him; although they declare themselves to be his servants, their service is no more than pretence.[48]

Contemplation

What aspects and attitudes in your life reflect the character of Christ? Your love for others shown in the life you live is the greatest reflection of Christ.

What fruit of a life centred on Christ does your life produce?

Would the name 'Christian' be given to you in its truest meaning by others due to your acts?

Reading

And this is his commandment, that we should believe in the name of his Son Jesus Christ and love one another, just as he has commanded us. All who obey his commandments abide in him, and he abides in them. And by this we know that he abides in us, by the Spirit that he has given us.

1 JOHN 3:23–24

Prayer

Loving God, as I endeavour to obey the commands of Christ, may your love flow through me. Give me more of your Spirit so that I can become even more like Christ. Amen

9 December

Patrick as a young man was brought up in a Christian family. He himself tells us at the beginning of the *Confession* that his father, Calpornius, was a deacon, and his grandfather, Potitus, was a presbyter. Yet as a young man, up until he was kidnapped by Irish raiders at the age of 16, Patrick tells us that he was disobedient to his Christian priests, and that he 'did not believe in the living God from [his] infancy'.[49] It was only after his capture that he became aware of his sense of unbelief and changed.

Patrick discovered the path back to his early teaching which he received as a boy but, more than that, he discovered a deep and extremely meaningful relationship with the Trinitarian God. He describes in his *Confession* his discovery of the Father, Son and Holy Spirit as separate, yet interwoven experiences. Patrick has a clear understanding of the theology of the Cosmic Christ, which we have already come across some days ago, as Patrick says in his *Confession*: 'Jesus Christ who was always with the Father... before the origin of the world, spiritually with the Father; in an inexplicable manner begotten before all beginning.'[50] Yet Patrick does not lose the depth of belief in the godhead, the Trinity, stating in the same section of the *Confession* that 'Jesus Christ is Lord *and God* in whom we believe and expect [his] coming'.[51]

As Patrick dwelled on the hills feeding and looking after the cattle, he began and practised what became a very deep abiding in God, in the divine presence. 'I prayed frequently during the day,' he says. 'The love of God and the fear of him increased more and more, and faith became stronger, and the spirit was stirred.'[52]

Patrick lived his whole life each day in this dwelling, or abiding, in God and the divine presence. It is clear through the way he lived his life, through his prayers and statements throughout his works and the missions which he later embarked on, that to him Jesus was the Son of the living God. It was this strength of belief which enabled him to become so close to God and to have the visions and dreams which he had, as well as the inner strength to return to the land of his captivity as a missionary after escaping. Patrick knew that he dwelled in God and that God dwelled in him, and it was this belief that empowered him to do all the amazing and miraculous things which have been passed down to us through the stories of his life.

Contemplation

How often do you confess that Jesus is the Son of God? Was it just a one-off confession when you said some form of prayer of conversion, or do you make that confession regularly?

Do you think it is important to reiterate this confession, like one might do during the saying of a creed, or do you think it is enough to just know it?

Reading

> And we have seen and do testify that the Father has sent his Son as the Saviour of the world. God abides in those who confess that Jesus is the Son of God, and they abide in God.
>
> 1 JOHN 4:14–15

Prayer

I believe in... Jesus Christ, [God's] only Son, our Lord: who was conceived by the Holy Spirit, born of the Virgin Mary; suffered under Pontius Pilate, was crucified, died and was buried. He descended into hell; the third day he rose again from the dead; he ascended into heaven, is seated at the right hand of God the Father Almighty; from thence he shall come to judge the living and the dead... Amen[53]

The third coming of Christ

This section of the 40 days is to ensure that our inner lives are ready for when Christ returns at the end of all things. Like the early church, the Celtic Christians believed that Christ would return at any moment, and so ensuring that we are ready to receive him is important.

10 December

This period of the 40 days is to ensure that each of us is ready to meet Christ when he returns; that our life is in the right state to encounter him. One of the ways in which those within the monastic centres did this was to live by the monastic rule. This was a way to ensure that you were keeping daily checks on how you behaved, keeping to a natural rhythm implemented not just into your day, but into your life as a whole. The monastic rule for the Celtic Christians, like everything else with their faith, was a holistic aspect of their life.

Having a rule of life is not very common these days for most Christians; however, there is a rise in the number of people joining and connecting to New Monastic communities.[54] These are often dispersed, but who have some form of rule or way of life, but it is still something of a minority. But you don't have to belong to one of these communities to have or desire to follow a rule. In his little book, *Keep it Simple*, Nick Page says,

> I do not want to romanticize the monastic life – it is hard and rigorous. Most of us don't want to enter a monastery. We are not interested in shaving our heads, wearing sandals and learning how to chant. We just want the world to slow down a little. But I do not need to become a monk to learn from them, to bring a little of their serenity and order into my life. It is possible to take a monastic approach to life without being a monk. All we have to do is create our own 'rule of life'. Your rule of life will be a statement of what you want out of life and, just as importantly, what you *don't* want out of life. Your rule will help you to decide what your priorities are and what kind of work you should do. It will help you to allocate your time, give

> priority to what is important, and get rid of all the stuff which makes life so cluttered.[55]

To have a rule of life is to put some structure into your daily walk with God. It isn't to restrict us, but actually to give some structure for better growth, a bit like the trellis for a garden plant.

Pelagius, whom we have already met in these 40 days, had some wise comments to make about having a rule. He said:

> In a single day, we make so many decisions, we cannot possibly weigh up the good and evil consequences of each decision. We are liable to make foolish and wrong decisions. For this reason, we need a rule, a simple set of moral principles that we can apply to each decision we make. This will not be foolproof, but with a good rule, our decision will far more often be right than wrong. Another reason for a rule is this: Jesus tells us to pray always; yet sometimes we love to devote much time to prayer whereas at other times we are dry or feel far too busy to pray. A rule prevents us from making excuses; it spurs us to pray at a particular time even when our heart is cold towards God.[56]

Here, Pelagius tells us that not only is a rule helpful for keeping our decision-making good, but also that it keeps us dedicated to spiritual disciplines even when we don't feel like it. If we are going to be ready for Christ when he returns, keeping to a rule or way of life is a good place to start.

Contemplation

> The teaching of Jesus must be the primary general guide for any disciple, but Jesus himself did not give rules. The source of the rule is inside your own heart. What we call conscience is a kind of rule which God has written on your heart. If you wish to formulate a rule you must listen to your conscience and write down on paper what God has written on your heart.[57]

Do you have a rule?

Do you keep spiritual disciplines? If not, perhaps you could take Pelagius' advice and begin by sitting quietly and contemplating what is in your heart.

Reading

> But know this: if the owner of the house had known at what hour the thief was coming, he would not have let his house be broken into. You also must be ready, for the Son of Man is coming at an unexpected hour.
> LUKE 12:39–40

Prayer

God of order and spiritual discipline, in my desire to live more focused on you and to become more like you even in the times when I do not feel like it, help me to keep the commitment to my rule, my way of life, so that I can be as ready for your return as I can be. Amen

11 December

As Beuno lay on his deathbed, he had a vision of heaven opening up above him. He saw the Trinity – the Father, Son and Holy Spirit – some of the apostles and other characters from the Bible, and angels. In the midst of the angels, he says:

> I saw seven angels standing before the throne of the highest Father and all the fathers of heaven singing: 'Blessed is the one you have chosen and have received and who shall dwell with you always.' I hear the cry of the horn of the highest Father summoning me and saying to me: 'My son, cast off your burden of flesh. The time is coming, and you are invited to share the feast [with your brothers] that shall not end. May your body remain in earth while the armies of heaven and the angels bear your soul to the kingdom of heaven, which you have merited here through your works.'[58]

Beuno was invited in to the wedding feast, to the heavenly party, as he lay dying. He was a holy man who planted many monastic centres and churches but, more than this, he helped the poor, as well as leading kings to know Christ. In the *Life of Beuno*, we hear three times of him raising people from the dead by placing their decapitated heads back on to their bodies. The life of Beuno is short, as the writer felt that he didn't want to go on too much about how holy and amazing Beuno was 'in case [the] book should seem long-winded'.[59] But the biographer does tell us this:

> Beuno performed all the commandments of God. He gave food and drink to anyone who was hungry or thirsty, clothing for the naked, lodging for the stranger. He visited the sick and those

> in prison. He performed every good thing that holy scripture tells us to do.[60]

Beuno's life of doing good and following what God told him to do, of going where God told him to go and of fully obeying the word of God was the preparation for the heavenly party. It was because he lived a life as a Christian in the way scripture tells us to (compare the list of good deeds above with those found in Matthew 25:31–46) that he was invited into the wedding feast in eternity. The bridegroom arrived and Beuno was prepared; his life was the oil for his lamp.

Contemplation

In what way do you live out the call found in Matthew 25:31–46?

How is your life an example of being prepared for the call into the heavenly party, the wedding feast?

Beuno's life was simply one given over to God and filled with the desire to do what God called him to do, be that visiting those who were sick or raising decapitated people back to life. When we give our lives fully over to God, there is no limit to what God can do through us. Spend time with God contemplating what it would mean for you to give your life over fully to God.

Reading

> Then the kingdom of heaven will be like this. Ten bridesmaids took their lamps and went to meet the bridegroom. Five of them were foolish, and five were wise. When the foolish took their lamps, they took no oil with them; but the wise took flasks of oil with their lamps. As the bridegroom was delayed, all of them became drowsy and slept. But at midnight there was a shout, 'Look! Here is the bridegroom! Come out to meet him.'

Then all those bridesmaids got up and trimmed their lamps. The foolish said to the wise, 'Give us some of your oil, for our lamps are going out.' But the wise replied, 'No! there will not be enough for you and for us; you had better go to the dealers and buy some for yourselves.' And while they went to buy it, the bridegroom came, and those who were ready went with him into the wedding banquet; and the door was shut. Later the other bridesmaids came also, saying, 'Lord, lord, open to us.' But he replied, 'Truly I tell you, I do not know you.' Keep awake therefore, for you know neither the day nor the hour.

MATTHEW 25:1–13

Prayer

Loving Bridegroom, you call me to be ready. I prepare myself for the invitation to the wedding feast by the life I live, by following your commands both in scripture and in my own heart. Help me to be ready. Amen

12 December

We don't often think of great signs and wonders happening as directional indications or warnings from God. Another of the downsides of living in a 'post-Enlightenment' culture and in a scientific age is that we dismiss natural phenomena as simply natural things happening around us. We never think that it might be a sign from God, or that God might even put signs in the natural world for us, or cause things to happen in the natural world as signs for us.

In ancient cultures, the natural world was simply a canvas, a blank page, for God to be able to write upon to give us signs and to speak to us through it. The natural world was seen as having God as part of it, as interacting with it, so as much as God could send an angel to speak to us, or speak to us directly, he could also use natural phenomena or any aspect of the natural world to speak directly to us.

The natural world was one way in which God could give us warnings: warnings of things happening in the future; warnings of disasters or some catastrophe, so that those who were able to discern, or perhaps simply those who were willing to believe that God might speak through these signs, could be ready and be warned.

In the *Anglo-Saxon Chronicles*, which we have already encountered in these 40 days, there is an example of these signs and wonders. It comes as a precursor to the invasion of the Vikings. Lindisfarne was the first place in Britain on which the Vikings stepped foot. But before they arrived there were signs and warnings in the natural world:

> AD 793. This year came dreadful forewarnings over the land of the Northumbrians, terrifying the people most woefully:

> there were immense sheets of light rushing through the air, and whirlwinds, and fiery dragons flying across the firmament. These tremendous tokens were soon followed by a great famine, and not long after, on the sixth day before the ides of January in the same year, the harrowing inroads of heathen men made lamentable havoc in the church of God in Holy-Island, by rapine and slaughter. Siga died on the eighth day before the calends of March.[61]

In the same way, Jesus tells his disciples that there will be warnings before Christ returns. Signs in the natural world to give a prewarning that Christ is about to come back. Will you be ready?

Contemplation

How do you view the natural world? Do you see it as just a physical place?

Maybe you do believe that God is within it, but do you believe that God can use it to speak to you? To warn you?

Have you ever had the experience where things have happened in the natural creation which you have taken as a sign or warning from God? Why/why not?

Reading

> [The Coming of the Son of Man] There will be signs in the sun, the moon, and the stars, and on the earth distress among nations confused by the roaring of the sea and the waves.
>
> LUKE 21:25

Prayer

Creator God, God who interacts with your creation, may I see your hand and presence within the natural world around me. May I also be open to you using the natural world to speak to me, and to send warnings and words to me so that I can know your guidance. Amen

13 December

Death is something most people in the western world do not like to talk about. There is, in many people, a fear of death, and so we avoid the subject. But for the Christian there should be no fear in death; there should be no desire to hide from it and not include it in conversation, because for the Christian there is no death, just a transference of existence.

The body we currently use, which we feel and touch and others see when we are with them, will no longer function. It will give out like a drained battery, but the essence of who we are, our soul and spirit, the real, 'true' self – that will just carry on in a different realm and level of existence.

For the Celtic Christians, not only was there no fear in death, but they would actively seek out what they called their place of resurrection. The place where, at the end of time when Christ returns to recall those who loved him, they would rise into the air from their physical grave to be with him. This place of resurrection was a significant place.

The land, the very earth on which they lived, was special and sacred to the Celtic peoples, including the Celtic Christians. The phrase 'thin place' is one which we gain from the Celtic idea of the significance of place. So why would it be any different with regards to the place in which they would die and their body would be buried?

One of the accounts we have with regards to this idea of the place of resurrection comes from the *Book of Lismore*. In this book, we discover that a sixth-century hermit named Canaire had a vision when she was in her hermitage. She saw a tower of fire rise up from every church and monastic centre in Ireland. The tower of fire from Senán mac Geircinn's monastery at Inis Cathaig, in the mouth of the Shannon River, however, was the highest, and the straightest towards heaven, so Canaire set off in that direction, deciding that it was the most holy.

Canaire appealed to God that she be buried on this most holy of islands, for it is there that she believed would be her place of resurrection.[62] So she set off, weakened by her advanced age, but driven by determination and faith, walking the whole way.

However, when she arrived, Senán was not impressed. He didn't want any women on the island. Canaire argued with him on the basis that Christ died for women as well as men, and that she had been given a vision of this place as her place of resurrection.

Although this was not the normal perspective of the Celtic saints towards women, Senán conceded the tiniest amount. He said that Canaire could have the edge of the island on which they currently stood. Canaire agreed and Senán led a Eucharist for them both. Following the Eucharist, Canaire died there on the beach, finding her place of resurrection, fulfilling her vision.

Contemplation

What do you think about death? Or are you one who avoids thinking and talking about it?

Where might your place of resurrection be? What special place, what thin place, would be your desire to have as the place from which you rose from in your resurrection body?

Reading

For since we believe that Jesus died and rose again, even so, through Jesus, God will bring with him those who have died. For this we declare to you by the word of the Lord, that we who are alive, who are left until the coming of the Lord, will by no means precede those who have died. For the Lord himself, with a cry of command, with the archangel's call and with the sound of God's trumpet, will descend from heaven, and the dead in Christ will rise first.

1 THESSALONIANS 4:14–16

Prayer

Holy God of all eternity, death has no sting for those who follow you, who believe in your words about resurrection and being with you. May I see 'death' as it simply is – a transference of existence from this mortal frame into a greater sense and dimension. May I find my place of resurrection. Amen

14 December

We are very impatient today. Instant gratification has become the expected norm for our modern, western culture. You don't have to wait for home cooked meals now; you can buy packets and put them in the microwave for a few minutes. You don't have to wait for food in a restaurant; you can go to a fast food place. You don't have to wait to get to a music shop to buy whatever album you want; you can download it immediately on to the device you have in your pocket. You don't have to wait to go to a book shop; you can download your book on to an ebook or other device. Even if you want to have a physical book, you can order whatever you want online and have it delivered the next morning. When I was young, the normal tag line on anything you ordered was: 'Please allow 28 days for delivery.' Most children these days wouldn't be able to wait 28 days for delivery; they would have moved on to the next thing by then! You don't even need to wait any more until you can afford something; you can have almost everything on hire-purchase.

Waiting is not an expected part of our modern, western culture.

This lack of waiting has bred in us the lack of patience, which is a natural by-product of not having to wait. But patience is such an important part of human development. Patience is what we strengthen by waiting, even if we wait in an active way rather than a passive way, like Advent is all about. We still wait. We grow in patience, not impatience.

In the *Life of David*, patron saint of Wales, we discover that patience was something which he took seriously:

> Whoever desired this saintly way of life and sought to enter the company of the brethren had first to remain for ten days outside the doors of the monastery, as if rejected and reduced to silence by words of abuse. If he exercised patience and stood there until the tenth day, he was first admitted and put to serve under the elder who had charge of the gate. When he had laboured there for a good while, and resistance in his soul had been broken down, he was finally judged to be ready to enter the company of the brethren.[63]

David did this to ensure that those who came to become a part of his monastic centres were absolutely certain that they really wanted to be a part of it: that they were called to come, and it wasn't just some whim.

David knew that endurance and patience were significantly important parts of what it meant to be a monk. To sit and wait on God needed to be practised by sitting and waiting in the physical world. Patience in the physical increased patience in the spiritual.

The same is true today. Perhaps if you struggle to wait on God, to sit and wait in meditation and contemplation, practise patience in some physical aspect of your life, to build up the resilience for the spiritual life, including the coming of Christ.

Contemplation

How patient are you? Is it one of the fruit of the Spirit which comes naturally to you? Or is it something you need to work on?

Perhaps you can think of ways in which you can exercise patience in the physical world so that it might increase your patience in dwelling with God.

Perhaps, if it is not urgent, you could do something as simple as waiting for a few days between seeing something you want and clicking 'buy' in an online shop, even if you do have the money.

Reading

> Be patient, therefore, beloved, until the coming of the Lord. The farmer waits for the precious crop from the earth, being patient with it until it receives the early and the late rains. You also must be patient. Strengthen your hearts, for the coming of the Lord is near.
>
> JAMES 5:7–8

Prayer

Ever-living God, God who is not restrained by time, grant me greater patience that I might wait on you – both in contemplation and stillness, but also to wait for your coming at the end of time. Like the farmer waits patiently for the crop, may I wait patiently for you. Amen

15 December

Today's reading is one which can be interpreted to suggest that we do not need to look after the earth because it will all be destroyed at the end of time anyway. Personally, I think there is more metaphor or poetic language in these words than literalism, and for me the important words are right there in the middle: 'What sort of persons ought you to be in leading lives of holiness and godliness?' That's the focal point, at least today. As we wait for Christ to return, what sort of people ought we to be? It seems obvious; in fact, the writer gives us (part of) the answer – *leading lives of holiness and godliness*. We should be people who, while waiting, strive to be the best we can be, not in our own strength, but in the divine strength working in and through us.

This concept of being the best people we can be, people living lives of holiness and godliness, can be seen in the lives of people throughout our Christian spiritual heritage, especially in the convents, monastic centres and deserts. The Celtic Christians were no exception to this. Many of the Celtic saints were described as having lived lives of such holy brilliance that it almost seems unreal, until we remember that this is about God working in the human, not anything which has been achieved by human effort. One of the greatest descriptions is of Aidan, founder of Lindisfarne. In his *Ecclesiastical History of the English People*, Bede describes Aidan like this:

> Bishop Aidan, a man of outstanding gentleness, devotion, and moderation, who had a zeal for God… Such were his love of peace and charity, temperance and humility; his soul which triumphed over anger and greed and at the same time despised pride and vainglory; his industry in carrying out and teaching

> the divine commandments, his diligence in study and keeping vigil, his authority, such as became a priest, in reproving the proud and the mighty, and his tenderness in comforting the weak, in relieving and protecting the poor.
>
> To put it briefly, so far as one can learn from those who knew him, he made it his business to omit none of the commands of the evangelists, the apostles and the prophets, but he set himself to carry them out in his deeds, so far as he was able. All these things I greatly admire and love in this bishop and I have no doubt that all this was pleasing to God… Aidan taught the clergy many lessons about the conduct of their lives… and the best recommendation of his teaching to all was that he taught them no other way of life than that which he himself practised among his fellows.[64]

This incredible accolade given to the founding bishop of Lindisfarne shows us that there was a great appreciation of the holiness and godliness of the lives of such saints. They were used as inspiration for those living after they had died (or transferred their existence!). The descriptions of the saints and their wonderful acts were written down so that people like you and me can read them and be inspired that here were these men and women, just normal men and women, who had allowed God to work mightily in them and through them.

Whether the wording of today's verses is metaphorical or literal, let us be inspired to focus on those central words about how we should be living while we wait for these things to happen.

Contemplation

Take a moment to be a little introspective – not self-critical, but self-inspective; not chastising ourselves, but simply allowing the Spirit to reveal to you where you have achieved such aspects of living, and where you could improve on your holiness and godliness through God's power.

Reading

But the day of the Lord will come like a thief, and then the heavens will pass away with a loud noise, and the elements will be dissolved with fire, and the earth and everything that is done on it will be disclosed.

Since all these things are to be dissolved in this way, what sort of persons ought you to be in leading lives of holiness and godliness, waiting for and hastening the coming of the day of God, because of which the heavens will be set ablaze and dissolved, and the elements will melt with fire? But, in accordance with his promise, we wait for new heavens and a new earth, where righteousness is at home.

2 PETER 3:10–13

Prayer

Holy God, moment by moment make me more and more like you. Increase the holiness and godliness within me. Amen

16 December

Brigid was born in Ireland to a noble family. As she grew to maturity, she worked churning the cows' milk to make butter. One day when she was doing so and had filled the containers, some poor wayfarers passed by. Brigid, always loving to follow the laws of God over human rules, gave away the butter she had churned to the poor. When the day was over a short time later, and it came to the time to present what she had made, Brigid opened her container expecting to have to explain why hers was empty, only to find that it was as full as it was before she had given the butter away.

On another occasion, when she was getting food ready for guests, she was moved with compassion to feed a stray dog with some of the pork which was being cooked for the visitors. When the time came to serve the guests their meal, it was found to have a full cut of pork in the pot. When she had a centre of her own, some lepers, knowing of her generous spirit and compassion, came to her asking for some beer, but Brigid did not have any beer to give them. Moved by compassion for them, she saw baths filled with water, over which she prayed. The water in the baths turned to beer and she gave the lepers not only the drink they wanted, but an opportunity for Brigid to show great hospitality to them also.

One time, Brigid, in her own community, was visited by a woman and her twelve-year-old daughter who had been dumb since birth. The young girl approached Brigid and we are told this:

> [Brigid], who was joyful and welcoming to all, encouraged her with words seasoned with divine salt and, following the example of our Saviour who commanded the little children to

> come to him, she took the daughter's hand in her own and, not knowing that the girl was dumb, asked her what it was that she desired.[65]

The girl's mother told Brigid that the girl was dumb and would not be able to answer. Brigid, however, told the girl's mother that she would not let go of the girl's hand until she gave an answer. Brigid then leaned gently towards the girl again and, with a smile, asked the girl again what it was that she wanted. The young girl immediately replied, 'I wish to do only what you desire of me.' The girl spoke from then on without any difficulties at all.

> The number of [Brigid's] miracles increased daily, so that they are now almost beyond counting, so many acts of pity and righteousness did she perform, answering the needs of the poor, whether it was convenient to do so or not.[66]

Contemplation

How we live, the orthopraxy of our faith, is as important as what we believe. Being like Christ is as important as believing in him in the first place.

Take a moment to reflect upon how you live your life. Just like yesterday, try not to be self-critical, but simply self-inspective; not chastising yourself, but simply discovering the reality of how you are living.

How might you become better in the compassionate orthopraxy of living a life like Christ?

Reading

Let the evildoer still do evil, and the filthy still be filthy, and the righteous still do right, and the holy still be holy.

See, I am coming soon; my reward is with me, to repay according to everyone's work. I am the Alpha and the Omega, the first and the last, the beginning and the end.

REVELATION 22:11–13

Prayer

Gracious and compassionate one, may I live a life which reflects your love and generosity to all. May I know your power moving through me so that your kingdom will come in the world in which I live. Amen

17 December

The Celtic Christians understood the spiritual realms to be as real and as active as the physical realm. They believed that there was an interweaving of these realms and that the angels were among us as we wander the earth, just in a different realm. Many of the Celtic saints would regularly converse with angels and would see them. On one occasion, when Columba was sitting in the scriptorium on Iona, he shouted a command which the monks with him did not understand. When they asked him what he meant, he replied that he was talking to the angel which he saw standing between them and was telling the angel to go and aid another monk in a different place.[67]

The concept of angelic protection was also something the Celtic Christians believed in: that the angels guard and protect us as we live our daily lives, as this was their heavenly charge.

The 19th/20th-century collection of Celtic prayers called the *Carmina Gadelica*, which reflect strongly what we know of the ancient Celtic church, includes certain prayers directed at angelic protection, more specifically to the archangel Michael. In scripture, Michael was the angel who fought battles in the heavenly realms (see, for example, Jude 9; Revelation 12:7–9), the militant angel within the battle in which we are 'not fighting against flesh-and-blood enemies, but against evil rulers and authorities of the unseen world, against mighty powers in this dark world, and against evil spirits in the heavenly places' (Ephesians 6:12, NLT). The Celtic Christians had prayers to call Michael to their aid, such as this one:

O Michael Militant, thou king of the angels, shield thy people with the power of thy sword,
shield thy people with the power of thy shield.
Spread thy wing over sea and land, east and west, and shield us from the foe, east and west from the foe.[68]

For the Celtic Christians, the angels, especially Michael, were there to help and protect us.

Contemplation

What is your view of angels? Do you see them as beings which exist around us but in a different realm – a world within our world, interwoven with our own?

Do you ask for angelic protection? Do you think you should/would?

Reading

> At that time Michael, the great prince, the protector of your people, shall arise. There shall be a time of anguish, such as has never occurred since nations first came into existence. But at that time your people shall be delivered, everyone who is found written in the book. Many of those who sleep in the dust of the earth shall awake, some to everlasting life, and some to shame and everlasting contempt. Those who are wise shall shine like the brightness of the sky, and those who lead many to righteousness, like the stars for ever and ever.
>
> DANIEL 12:1–3

Prayer

O Michael of the angels and the righteous in heaven, shield thou my soul with the shade of thy wing, shield thou my soul on earth and in heaven. From foes upon the earth, from foes beneath the earth, from foes in concealment protect and encircle my soul 'neath thy wing, oh my soul with the shade of thy wing.[69]

18 December

For the Celtic Christians, growing in knowledge and understanding was more than an intellectual endeavour; it was something which encapsulated the whole of life. This holistic view of the world and their faith was a thread which spread throughout the whole of their world and spiritual outlook. Relationship was at the heart of this. Relationship with each other, and a particular 'other': in the Celtic languages, an *anam chara*, a Soul Friend. The Soul Friend would be one with whom you could learn about life and faith by building a relationship with them by becoming open and vulnerable in their love and knowing that they wanted what was best for you. This way, you were more able to live a life of purity and righteousness, where you would see the fruit of your internal labour as you cultivated, with your Soul Friend, your soul and spirit, as well as every aspect of your physical and practical life.

If the focus of this time, anticipating the last coming of Christ, was to ensure that one's life was in a state of readiness for when Christ returns, then the Soul Friend was indispensable.

A phrase which comes from the Celtic Christian heritage shows the importance laid on an *anam chara*. It states that a person without a Soul Friend is like a body without a head. Edward Sellner[70] attributes this phrase to Brigid (d. 523), as does Ray Simpson,[71] after she saw the head of a cleric disappear as he ate, taking this as prophecy that his Soul Friend had that moment died.[72] George Metlake in his book *The Life and Writings of St Columban*, however, attributes it to Comgall (d. 602).[73] Whoever may have said it first, if either of them at all, what we can deduce by this phrase being a part of the Celtic legacy is that the practice of having a Soul Friend was an important part of the ongoing transformation, or discipleship, of the people within the Celtic Church. However, as Edward Sellner also says in *The Celtic Soul Friend*:

> The belief that there are relationships that can be especially helpful for personal growth and the acquisition of wisdom is not unique to the Celts or Celtic lands. Teachers, mentors and benevolent helpers have been identified in many spiritual traditions in the history of humankind. The philosopher of the Greeks, the shaman of the native tribes, the Rabbi of the Jews, the guru of the Hindus, the Zen Master of the Buddhists, the *staretz* of Eastern Orthodox Christians – all are considered by their followers as important resources for their spirituality. Still, the *anam chara* of the early Celtic church has a unique value of its own, for it came to be closely associated in Christianity with ongoing transformation, a process of conversion-reconciliation that included frequent disclosure to a soul friend.[74]

The love that is evident between Soul Friends in the lives of the Celtic saints, and the relationship which they had to help the other grow in knowledge and wisdom, truly enabled the Celtic Christians to live lives of purity and to bear fruit of righteousness as they ensured that they were ready for the coming of Christ at the end of all things.

Contemplation

Do you have a Soul Friend? Do you have someone to whom you are open and vulnerable to enable you to grow in your life and faith? If you do, then pause to reflect on how they have helped you in your life journey so far. If you do not, then pause and consider who you might know who could fulfil that role for you in your life journey.

Reading

I pray that your love will overflow more and more, and that you will keep on growing in knowledge and understanding. For I want you to understand what really matters, so that you may live pure and blameless lives until the day of Christ's return. May you always be filled with the fruit of your salvation – the righteous character produced in your life by Jesus Christ – for this will bring much glory and praise to God.

PHILIPPIANS 1:9–11 (NLT)

Prayer

Loving heavenly Father, brother Christ, Holy Spirit helper, thank you for the love and relationship I have with you. May I share that same love in relationship with my *anam chara*, my Soul Friend. May I know the help of another to live a life of holiness and purity, that I too can ensure that my inner self is ready for your return. Amen

19 December

Before Patrick went to Ireland, Christianity already existed there. Churches and monastic centres grew, mainly in the south, and the message of Christ was preached among the tribes and clans.

At Tara, the centre of the High Kings of Ireland, in the mid-fourth century, the Déisi tribe was banished after a skirmish with the king. Some of them then fled to live in hiding; some of them returned to Tara, repentant. Yet some others went to the south-east of Ireland to start a new life, intermarrying with another tribe. The story of the Déisi tribal skirmish was told in the epic tales of the Irish bards.

Within this new land, Déclán was born into a Christian family and baptised. At the age of seven, he was presented to the local holy man, who taught him to read, write and keep the hours of monastic prayer. Déclán went to study abroad and, when he returned, he carried a monk's bell and staff – signs that he was ordained and ready to plant his own centres, the first of which he planted in 416.

Déclán travelled around the local towns and villages, strengthening the faith of the local Christians with signs and wonders and eloquent words. He performed miracles and blessed holy wells, which then healed those who drank from their water.

Déclán, like most of the Celtic monks, loved to spend time in solitude to strengthen his own faith through contemplative prayer and prolonged periods of silence.

He built a hermitage in the wood close to his monastic centre so that he could escape the busy monastic life and go to spend time with

God. Déclán referred to this place as his 'desert' – a place of emptiness and stillness and quiet – after the inspiration of the Desert Fathers and Mothers, who were a great influence on the whole of the Celtic church.

Déclán's future missions came from his times of silence and stillness. He would draw into the deep presence of God which then enabled him to pour out what he gained from contemplation in his ministry and mission. Déclán was a man who took time to strengthen his own inner self, before he went out to encourage and strengthen those who came to hear him who were followers of Christ.

Contemplation

How much time do you spend in quiet contemplation? What value do you place on dwelling in stillness with God? Do you think this is a good way to prepare to go out and allow the Spirit of God to flow through you?

Spend time with God now, just sitting and being. No words. No thoughts. Just sitting and being.

Reading

> Just as the testimony of Christ has been strengthened among you – so that you are not lacking in any spiritual gift as you wait for the revealing of our Lord Jesus Christ. He will also strengthen you to the end, so that you may be blameless on the day of our Lord Jesus Christ.
>
> 1 CORINTHIANS 1:6–8

Prayer

Come before God in silence.

Celebrating the Christmas feast and winter celebrations

20 December

In the ancient British and Irish calendars, from the beginning of November to the end of January was the winter season, the season of death and darkness, as the world around you seems to die. The trees and plants, and even the disappearance of many animals and birds either into hibernation or simply hiding from the cold, can make the earth seem quite dead. In the pre-Christian era, the season got its name from the god of the darkness – Samhain (pronounced *sah-wen*).

In the Roman and Anglo-Saxon eras, the months that correspond with December and January were collectively known as *Giuli*, a Germanic word from which we get the word 'Yule'. Bede, in his book *On the Reckoning of Time*, implies that *Geola* (Yule) was the name for the period in which the winter solstice occurs, and he states that these months 'derive their name from the day when the Sun turns back to increase, because one precedes and the other follows'.

However, judging by the names of the months, it's equally possible that *Geola* was the name for the whole midwinter season. December was *Ærra Geola*, which can be interpreted as either 'first Yule' or 'preceding Yule', and January was *Æfterra Geola*, 'following Yule', or 'after Yule'. There was also a great influence in Britain and Ireland from the Norse cultures. In Norse, the word *Jol* is the corresponding word, very close to *Geola*. *Geola* is possibly Germanic, from a source akin to the Old Norse *Jol* which was a winter festive time.

These words, some suggest, have the same root as the modern English word 'jolly', suggesting the festive aspect of the season – a celebration, which may have included the Yule Log, although the earliest direct reference to a Yule Log doesn't come until the 17th century.

Whatever the true history is, it seems that our ancient ancestors draw out a sense of celebration from the season of death and darkness, something which we still do nowadays: an ancient custom which has always existed right up until today!

Contemplation

How do you view the winter season? Does the darkness overwhelm you? Do you feel like celebrating? Our ancestors understood that long, dark days for a whole season could become overwhelmingly oppressive. They created festivities to lift their spirits. Spend time with God now in praise and thanksgiving for all the good things. Don't let the darkness be the focus.

Reading

> The Lord spoke to Moses, saying: 'Speak to the people of Israel and say to them: These are the appointed festivals of the Lord that you shall proclaim as holy convocations.'
>
> LEVITICUS 23:1–2

> It was now winter, and Jesus was in Jerusalem at the time of Hanukkah, the Festival of Dedication. He was in the Temple, walking through the section known as Solomon's Colonnade.
>
> JOHN 10:22–23 (NLT)

Prayer

God of joy and celebration, thank you that, even in the midst of the darkness, we can celebrate light. We know that you brought festivals into the lives of your people, and you still want us to enjoy ourselves. May I know a sense of divine joy as I celebrate this season. Amen

21 December

As we mentioned yesterday, this whole season was one in which darkness seemed to prevail. However, darkness was not the focus for the season. As well as the element of joy in Yule, right in the centre of this dark cold season was the winter solstice, one of the eight points of the ancient calendar which the early Celtic saints would have followed.

The winter solstice, which shifts a little each year as it is based on the actual movements of the sun and moon instead of any modern calendar, is the day upon which the light of the sun shines for the shortest amount of time. The word 'solstice' literally means 'sun stand still', from the words 'sol' – sun – and the past participle stem of 'sistere' – to stand still. There is a moment in the movement of the sun (or, more correctly the movement of the earth) where the sun seems to stand still, and not move in the sky, just for the briefest moment, as it begins to turn, a bit like when you throw a ball into the air and it stops for the briefest moment between going up and coming down. For this briefest moment, it is 'sol-stice'.

Even though the winter solstice was the time when the sun shone for the least amount of time in the middle of the season of darkness, for the ancient Celts this was not a celebration of darkness, or even a focus on darkness. Even the pre-Christian Celts used physical things as metaphors for spiritual truths, and so the focus of the winter solstice was, and is, not the darkness. Instead, the focus is the fact that, from this moment onwards, the light begins to grow in strength and become stronger, overcoming the darkness, as it makes its way to the opposite point in the year, the summer solstice: the longest period of sunlight in the sky, when the sun is at its strongest.

The focus of the winter solstice is the light overpowering the darkness – a metaphor which we, as Christians, can relate to fully. As we reach this midpoint in the winter season, just a few days before Christmas, we can stop and pause in the darkness and remember that the light comes to overcome and overpower the darkness, that the darkness does not have any power because of the light of the world, Jesus Christ.

Contemplation

Pause for a moment and contemplate darkness. What is darkness? Darkness is not actually a thing. You can't switch it on, and it only exists when there is a lack of light. To dispel darkness, simply increase the light. You can switch the light on, because light is a thing, but darkness is not; darkness is just the lack of that thing – the light.

What might this physical reality mean to you in a spiritual context in your own inner life? And the life of the world in which we live?

Reading

> The light shines in the darkness, and the darkness did not overcome it... The true light, which enlightens everyone, was coming into the world.
>
> JOHN 1:5, 9

> I have told you all this so that you may have peace in me. Here on earth you will have many trials and sorrows. But take heart, because I have overcome the world.
>
> JOHN 16:33 (NLT)

Prayer

Warmth of all warmth, comfort of all comfort, be with me this day. I would share your warmth with others, and be to the other that which the Great Other is to me.

Let not the darkness overcome us, but let the light shine from within to illuminate that which is darkness.

As the darkness stretches its long hand over this land, let your Light shine forth from within your people, that none would be left in darkness, but that instead we will live in the hope of the coming Light.

Great Light, be my guide. Hold me fast in this present darkness that I may be the fire on a hilltop in this dark time. Burn within me, now and ever more.[75]

22 December

Bede, best known for his *Ecclesiastical History of the English People* also wrote a treatise called *On the Reckoning of Time* with the purpose of explaining how the dates of Christian festivals were calculated. In this book, he includes a chapter on 'The English Months', by which he means the months that the 'heathen' English observed before they adopted the Roman ('Christian') calendar. In doing so, he preserved some old Anglo-Saxon lore which would otherwise have been lost.

According to Bede, the year began on *Modranecht*, or 'Mothers' Night', which was observed on 25 December 'when we celebrate the birth of our Lord'. There has been a lot of speculation by both Christian scholars and pagan authors as to who or what the 'mothers' in this word refers. Many believe the Anglo-Saxons would have honoured Germanic female ancestral spirits known as the *Idisi* on this day, but no conclusive proof has been found either way.

What we can take from this, wherever the source and origin comes from, is the fact that, for these ancient peoples of the Celtic and Anglo-Saxon nations, the role of 'mother' was an important one, one which was celebrated, whether that be our own mother, a spiritual mother or any metaphorical ones. Perhaps this sense and expression was what was behind 'Hild' (Hilda of Whitby) becoming known as the 'mother of the church'. Bede tells us this:

> All who knew Hild, the handmaiden of Christ and abbess, used to call her mother because of her outstanding devotion and grace. She was not only an example of holy life to all who were in the monastery but she also provided an opportunity for

> salvation and repentance to many who lived far away and who heard the happy story of her industry and virtue.[76]

The kind and loving character we see in the story of Hilda's life shows us that there really was a deep maternal instinct within her. It may well be that in the first half of her life she had a husband and even children. She was a princess and so would probably have been married before she was 30, and she is not referred to as a virgin, as many other women who took the habit were. So perhaps she had this experience of being a mother in real life, in the physical sense, and not just in a metaphorical sense. If Hilda ever was married and had children, it would seem that they must have died, perhaps in battle, at some point. Perhaps this was what prompted her at 33 to become a nun.

Whether or not Hilda had a husband and children of her own, her maternal instincts were certainly evident in her ministry: the way she nurtured and encouraged Cædmon, for example.

The role of mother, it seems, was important and significant to the ancient Celtic and Anglo-Saxon culture. Perhaps we could learn something from this for ourselves today, not just physically, but in the way in which we foster people spiritually, how we encourage and nurture them.

Contemplation

Take a moment to reflect and remember the women who have been influential in your life, whether that be your own mother, or any other women who have helped you along life's path and in your spiritual growth.

Thank God for them now.

Reading

The angel Gabriel was sent by God to a town in Galilee called Nazareth, to a virgin engaged to a man whose name was Joseph, of the house of David. The virgin's name was Mary... 'You have found favour with God. And now, you will conceive in your womb and bear a son, and you will name him Jesus... The Holy Spirit will come upon you, and the power of the Most High will overshadow you; therefore the child to be born will be holy; he will be called Son of God'... Then Mary said, 'Here am I, the servant of the Lord; let it be with me according to your word.' Then the angel departed from her.

In those days Mary set out and went with haste to a Judean town in the hill country, where she entered the house of Zechariah and greeted Elizabeth. When Elizabeth heard Mary's greeting, the child leapt in her womb. And Elizabeth was filled with the Holy Spirit and exclaimed with a loud cry, 'Blessed are you among women, and blessed is the fruit of your womb... And blessed is she who believed that there would be a fulfilment of what was spoken to her by the Lord.'

And Mary said, 'My soul magnifies the Lord, and my spirit rejoices in God my Saviour, for he has looked with favour on the lowliness of his servant. Surely, from now on all generations will call me blessed; for the Mighty One has done great things for me, and holy is his name.'

LUKE 1:26–49 (abridged)

Prayer

Loving God, who is beyond gender, and so can be my heavenly Mother as well as my heavenly Father, may I know your Mother's love this day, may I know that wonderful connection that is only possible between a mother and her child between you and me. Be with me this day, O wonderful Mother God. Amen

23 December

Exchanging gifts is a big part of the modern Christmas tradition. Although this is based mostly upon St Nicholas (who has not been mentioned, as he was not a Celtic saint), it also has links with elements of the Norse god Odin, and some Christians relate the tradition of gift giving with the gifts of the magi to Christ at his birth. However the tradition came about, the sense of generosity which abounds at this time of year between people is a wonderful thing. But generosity and the heart of giving should not just be kept for the Christmas season, but should be a part of our spirit in everyday life.

There are many stories of the generosity of the Celtic saints. Perhaps the most famous saint for generosity was Brigid of Kildare. But there are many other stories.

As Ciarán of Clonmacnoise lay dying, he was visited by his Soul Friend, Kevin of Glendalough. At the end of their exchange, just before Ciarán died, he gave Kevin his monk's bell. Many monks had their own small bell, and Ciarán wanted Kevin to have his so that he would have a gift to remember him by.

Two of the most influential saints in Scotland, Columba of Iona, and Kentigern of Glasgow once met one another. They spent hours together talking and, when they got up to depart from one another's company, they exchanged gifts. Kentigern gave Columba his pastoral staff, and Columba gave Kentigern *his* pastoral staff. Each now took the powerful emblem of the other away with them.

The giving of gifts can be one of the deepest and most moving of experiences. If we give from the heart, it doesn't matter how expensive the gift is, neither does it really matter what the gift is at all; what matters is that the spirit of generosity has been stirred in one person to give something to another.

Gifts don't even have to be physical things; there is much of ourselves and our time which can be given to others also. While we should ensure that we do not overdo that giving of ourselves and our time to our detriment, these gifts can oftentimes be received with more gratitude than any physical gift you can give.

Contemplation

This spirit of generosity should not just be restricted to Christmas, or birthdays, but should be a part of who we are as Christians every day of our lives.

As you give your gifts this Christmas, contemplate why you are doing it. Think about whether this is something which stirs within you at Christmas, or whether this is something which is a part of who you are in your everyday walk with God. If it is not, then contemplate why, and ask God to give you the spirit of generosity.

Reading

> Now concerning spiritual gifts, brothers and sisters, I do not want you to be uninformed. You know that when you were pagans, you were enticed and led astray to idols that could not speak. Therefore I want you to understand that no one speaking by the Spirit of God ever says 'Let Jesus be cursed!' and no one can say, 'Jesus is Lord' except by the Holy Spirit.
>
> Now there are varieties of gifts, but the same Spirit; and there are varieties of services, but the same Lord; and there are varieties of activities, but it is the same God who activates all of them in everyone. To each is given the manifestation of

the Spirit for the common good. To one is given through the Spirit the utterance of wisdom, and to another the utterance of knowledge according to the same Spirit, to another faith by the same Spirit, to another gifts of healing by the one Spirit, to another the working of miracles, to another prophecy, to another the discernment of spirits, to another various kinds of tongues, to another the interpretation of tongues. All these are activated by one and the same Spirit, who allots to each one individually just as the Spirit chooses.

1 CORINTHIANS 12:1–11

Prayer

Generous one, thank you for all the gifts you give to me. Thank you for all the gifts I have been given by others. Please open up in me more the spirit of generosity so that I can give gifts to others with joy and gladness simply from the act of giving. Amen

24 December

So we reach the final day, the night before Christmas! When we settle into our beds and the wait for the celebration is over, our Advent has come to an end.

This night, we enter rest ready to rise to the celebration of the birth of the Messiah, the Christ, Immanuel, God with us. The incarnation has taken place, we have readied ourselves to celebrate; not only this, but we have contemplated the coming of Christ within us, into our own lives, and we have readied ourselves for the coming again of Christ at the end of all things.

> *This night is the long night… white moon there will be till morn.*
> *This night is the eve of the Great Nativity, this night is born Mary Virgin's Son, this night is born Jesus, Son of the King of glory.*
> *This night is born the root of our joy, this night gleamed the sun of the mountains high, this night gleamed sea and shore together.*
> *This night was born Christ the King of greatness.*
> *Ere it was heard that the Glory was come, heard was the wave upon the strand; ere 'twas heard that His foot had reached the earth, heard was the song of the angels glorious.*
> *This night is the long night.*[77]

As we settle down ready for tomorrow's celebrations, we remember all that the Celtic Christian tradition has taught us about the celebration of Christmas, about the sense of Advent and the 40 days we have focused upon Christ. This night, for hundreds of years, our spiritual and physical ancestors have settled into their beds ready to greet the dawn on Christmas day and sing and celebrate with joy: **Emmanuel – GOD IS WITH US!**

Contemplation

As the time of Advent comes to an end, reflect back over the past 40 days. Reread any parts you wish to be reminded of once again; reread any notes you may have made. Then settle into peace, ready to rise in the morning to celebrate the coming of the Christ.

Reading

For a child has been born for us,
  a son given to us;
authority rests upon his shoulders;
  and he is named
Wonderful Counsellor, Mighty God,
  Everlasting Father, Prince of Peace.
His authority shall grow continually,
  and there shall be endless peace
for the throne of David and his kingdom.
  He will establish and uphold it
with justice and with righteousness
  from this time onward and for evermore.
The zeal of the Lord of hosts will do this.
ISAIAH 9:6–7

Prayer

Holy, gracious and loving God, you stepped into our world; you became incarnate; you took on our humanity that we might take on your divinity. May I rest this night knowing what the dawn brings, knowing the joy which awaits me. May I rest this night ready to celebrate the glorious birth of Jesus Christ. Amen

Nollaig shona daoibh!

'Nolag – shona – dov'

(Happy Christmas!)

Notes

1 Oliver Davies, *Celtic Spirituality* (Paulist Press, 1999), p. 156.
2 Davies, *Celtic Spirituality*, p. 157.
3 Davies, *Celtic Spirituality*, p. 158.
4 David Adam, *Aidan, Bede, Cuthbert: Three inspirational saints* (SPCK, 2006), pp. 33–34.
5 Refer, for example, to Ben Mackworth-Pread, *The Book of Kells* (Random House, 1997), plate IX.
6 See Brian Wright, *Brigid: Goddess, druidess and saint* (The History Press, 2009). 'Hebridean Story' is about Brigid 'the midwife of Mary', p. 90.
7 Bede, *The Ecclesiastical History of the English People* (Oxford University Press, 1999), Book 4, chapter 24.
8 I look at *The Dream of the Rood* in more detail in my book *Celtic Lent* (BRF, 2018).
9 Bede, 'The Life of St Cuthbert', found in Bertram Colgrave (trans.), *Two Lives of Saint Cuthbert* (Christ the King Library Publishing, undated), chapter 7.
10 Bede, 'Life of St Cuthbert', chapter 7.
11 Graham Panes, *Voyages of the Celtic Saints* (Gwasg Carreg Gwalch Publishers, 2007), pp. 7, 11.
12 *Anglo-Saxon Chronicle* (CODA books, 2012), p. 114.
13 Bede, *The Ecclesiastical History of the English People*, Book IV, chapter 23, p. 213.
14 Bede, 'The Life of St Cuthbert', chapter 6.
15 William Shakespeare, *Twelfth Night*, Act 2, Scene 5.
16 Anonymous, *Life of St Cuthbert*, Book 1, chapter 3.
17 Anonymous, *Life of St Cuthbert*, Book 1, chapter 3.
18 For example: 'Accepting their [the Magi's] authority would be tantamount to conversion to Zoroastrianism' and 'Magi (Zoroastrian priests)', *The Talmud: A selection* (Penguin Classics, 2009), pp. xxvii, 274.
19 Adamnan, *Life of Saint Columba* (George Routledge & Sons, 1939), p. 68.

20 Adamnan, *Life of Saint Columba*, p. 69.
21 Kenneth McIntosh (ed.), *The Winged Man: The good news according to Matthew (Celtic Bible Commentary)* (Anamchara Books, 2017), p. 90–91 (italics original).
22 Thomas O'Loughlin, *Celtic Theology* (Continuum Publishing, 2005), p. 97.
23 Christopher Bamford, *The Voice of the Eagle: The heart of Celtic Christianity* (Lindisfarne Books, 2000), p. 109.
24 Bamford, *The Voice of the Eagle*, p. 109.
25 Bamford, *The Voice of the Eagle*, p. 315.
26 See the 'Parable of the prisoner' in my book *Passing the Harp* (Anamchara Books, 2015).
28 Bamford, *The Voice of the Eagle*, p. 318.
29 Bamford, *The Voice of the Eagle*, p. 319.
20 From Thayer Definition in 'Strong's Concordance Lite'. G1787. '1. Within, inside. a. within you, i.e. in the midst of you; b. within you, i.e. your soul.'
30 Taken from 'Session 8: Warrior peacemakers' from the Celtic Christian Spirituality Correspondence Course run by Waymark Ministries. See waymarkministries.com/celtic-e-course.
31 Bede, *The Ecclesiastical History of the English People*, Book 4, chapter 25.
32 Bede, *The Ecclesiastical History of the English People*, Book 4, chapter 25, p. 220.
33 Thomas Taylor, *The Life of Samson of Dol* (Kessinger Legacy reprints, 1925), p. 50.
34 Taylor, *The Life of Samson of Dol*, p. 50.
35 This version is taken from Pat Robson, *A Celtic Liturgy* (Harper Collins, 2000), p. 55.
36 Taken from St Patrick's breastplate prayer.
37 Alexander Carmichael, *Carmina Gadelica* (Floris Books, 2006), pp. 204–05.
38 Extract taken from the song 'Everything' by Tim Hughes. Copyright © 2005 Thankyou Music. Adm. by Capitol CMG Publishing worldwide excl. UK & Europe, admin by Integrity Music, part of the David C Cook family, songs@integritymusic.com.
39 David Cole, *40 Days with the Celtic Saints* (BRF, 2017).
40 From Hugh Owen, 'Llanddwyn Island' in 'Transactions of the Anglesey Antiquarian Society and Field Club'. See tpwilliams.co.uk/newborough/hanes_pdf_ch8e_1.pdf, p. 6.

41 Found in Robson, *A Celtic Liturgy*, pp. 19–20.
42 Adapted from Romans 1:20 (*The Message*).
43 For a thorough explanation of the Stowe Missal, see its chapter in O'Loughlin, *Celtic Theology*.
44 Davies, *Celtic Spirituality*, pp. 316–17.
45 Taken from the Celtic Communion service found in Ray Simpson, *Liturgies from Lindisfarne* (Kevin Mayhew, 2010), p. 360.
46 James P. Mackey, *An Introduction to Celtic Christianity* (T&T Clark, 1995), pp. 389–90.
47 B.R. Rees, *Pelagius: Life and letters* (The Boydell Press, 2004), pp. 112–13.
48 Davies, *Celtic Spirituality*, pp. 380–81.
49 Patrick's *Confession*, taken from Noel Dermot O'Donoghue, *Aristocracy of the Soul* (DLT, 1987), p. 108.
50 O'Donoghue, *Aristocracy of the Soul*, p. 102.
51 O'Donoghue, *Aristocracy of the Soul*, p. 102 (italics mine).
52 O'Donoghue, *Aristocracy of the Soul*, p. 105.
53 Taken from the Apostle's Creed.
54 I belong to the Community of Aidan and Hilda. To find out more, visit aidanandhilda.org.uk.
55 Nick Page, *Keep it Simple (and get more out of life)* (Harper Collins, 1999), pp. 14–16.
56 Found in Ray Simpson, *Celtic Daily Light: A spiritual journey through the year* (Kevin Mayhew Publishing, 2003), 13 October.
57 Pelagius, quoted in Simpson, *Celtic Daily Light*, 13 October.
58 'The Life of Beuno', found in Davies, *Celtic Spirituality*, p. 220.
59 Davies, *Celtic Spirituality*, p. 219.
60 Davies, *Celtic Spirituality*, p. 219.
61 *Anglo-Saxon Chronicles*, pp. 89–91.
62 'Lives of the Saints' from the *Book of Lismore* (Llanerch publishing. 1995), pp. 219–20
63 Davies, *Celtic Spirituality*, p. 200.
64 Bede, *The Ecclesiastical History of the English People*, pp. 113, 137, 116.
65 Davies, *Celtic Spirituality*, p. 127.
66 Davies, *Celtic Spirituality*, pp. 127–28.
67 Adamnan, *Life of St Columba*, p. 209.
68 Carmichael, *Carmina Gadelica*, p. 235.
69 Carmichael, *Carmina Gadelica*, p. 236.
70 Edward Sellner, *The Celtic Soul Friend* (Ave Maria Press, 2002).

71 Ray Simpson, *Soul Friendship* (Hodder & Stoughton, 1999).

72 Edward C. Sellner, *The Celtic Soul Friend* (Ave Maria Press, 2002), p. 22: 'A young cleric of the community of Ferns, a foster son of Brigit's, used to come to her with dainties. He was often with her in the refectory to partake of food. Once after going to communion she strikes a clapper. "Well young cleric there," says Brigit, "do you have a soul friend?" "I have," replied the young man. "Let us sing his requiem," says Brigit. "Why so?" asks the young cleric. "For he has died," says Brigit. "When you had finished half your ration I saw that he was dead." "How did you know that?" "Easy to say," [Brigit replies] "from the time that your soul friend was dead, I saw your food was put [directly] in the trunk of your body, since you were without any head. Go forth and eat nothing until you get a soul friend, for anyone without a soul friend is like a body without a head: is like water of a polluted lake, neither good for drinking nor for washing. That is the person without a soul friend."'

73 George Metlake quotes H. D'Arbois' *Revue Celtique* in *The Life and Writings of St Columban* (J.M.F. Books, 1993), p. 113.

74 Sellner, *The Celtic Soul Friend*, p. 14.

75 The 'winter solstice' prayer taken from David Cole, *Celtic Prayers and Practices* (Anamchara Books, 2014), pp. 67–68.

76 Bede, *The Ecclesiastical History of the English People*, p. 212.

77 Carmichael, *Carmina Gadelica*, pp. 223–24.

This inspirational book takes the reader through the 40 days of Lent to the celebration of Easter through the eyes and beliefs of Celtic Christianity. Drawing on primary sources of pastoral letters, monastic rules and the theological teaching of the Celtic church, the author presents a different perspective on the cross of Christ and draws us to see our own life journeys with a new and transforming vision.

Celtic Lent
40 days of devotions to Easter
David Cole
978 0 85746 637 2 £8.99

brfonline.org.uk

40 DAYS
with the
CELTIC
SAINTS
DEVOTIONAL READINGS
FOR A TIME OF PREPARATION
DAVID COLE